LAW FIRM MARKETING:
Successfully Promoting and Building Your Small Firm or Solo Practice

Daniel B. Kennedy

Professional Publishing
Burr Ridge, Illinois
New York, New York

Editor-in-chief:	Jeffrey Krames
Project editor:	Paula M. Buschman
Production manager:	Bob Lange
Interior designer:	Mercedes Santos
Compositor:	Publishing Services, Inc.
Typeface:	11/13 Times Roman
Printer:	Quebecor Printing Book Press, Inc.

Library of Congress Cataloging-in-Publication Data

Kennedy, Daniel B.
    Law firm marketing : successfully promoting and building your small firm or solo practice / Daniel B. Kennedy.
       p.   cm.
    Includes index.
    ISBN 0-7863-0195-3
    1. Lawyers—United States—Marketing.   2. Legal services—United States—Marketing.   I. Title.
KF16.5.K46 1994
340'.068'8—dc20

94–144

Table of Contents

Why Should You Read This Book?

Are you a sole practitioner or a partner in a small law firm? If you are, I hope you have already asked yourself this question: What is my marketing plan?

Does that question take you off guard? If you don't have a plan, one with measurable goals that you strive to meet with the same intensity that you pursue your clients' interests, you may find yourself playing catch-up in the near future.

In the last seven years, large firms, most notably in San Francisco and Chicago, have been hiring full-time marketing professionals to help them attract and retain clients. Some use techniques that are purely defensive, to fend off the marketing efforts of competitive firms. Other efforts are carefully planned to claim larger shares in specific areas of the law. During those same seven years, membership in the National Law Firm Marketing Association has grown from 25 to more than 1,000.

In 1993, more than 500 of these marketers convened in San Francisco intent on "devising new ways to make more clients more dependent upon the lawyers the marketers are marketing," as *The New York Times* reported.

The *Times* article, which some law firm marketing professionals feel was written in too disparaging a manner, described one lawyer's attempt to gain new clients by donating a copy of Alan Deshowitz's book, *Chutzpah,* to a local library with his name and phone number on the front leaf. This perhaps overzealous lawyer claims to have netted four new clients in just four weeks. A clever trick, but not law firm marketing.

While still in its infancy, the reality of law firm marketing, the good and the bad, is apparent; it is here to stay. And the firms that grow and prosper in the highly competitive marketplace of providing legal services will be those that make marketing a priority.

What is law firm marketing? It is more than advertising, though some elements of advertising are included in a marketing plan. It is more than brochures and newsletters, though information-rich print communications with clients can be a valuable marketing tool. It is more than client-focused attitudes and behaviors, though putting the needs of the client first is perhaps the most important aspect of any successful marketing plan. It is more than community relations, public relations, and tracking the results of your work, and more than productivity and total quality management, though all are important to a successful marketing plan.

Marketing is all of these things and more. In a nutshell, it is all of the efforts that you must take to make your plan work. And, as a sole practitioner or partner in a small law firm, you are in an enviable position to begin planning for your firm's marketing future now. Unlike large firms, which may number into the hundreds of attorneys, paraprofessionals, and support personnel, you have less people to train, less cooks who might spoil the broth.

How do you begin? In business, conventional wisdom suggests that a successful plan begins with setting your goal, and then doing all that is necessary to obtain the desired results.

The same can be said of a marketing plan. You start with the end results you wish your marketing plan to achieve—your goals—and then plan your steps to reach those goals, while remaining flexible to the inevitable array of changes along the way—changing client needs, the changing marketplace, changing technology, and even changes in your goals.

In this book, you will learn how to set realistic goals for your practice development and how to meet them in a cost-effective manner. Marketing plans that are too expensive to implement are doomed to failure; they languish on the drawing boards.

You will also learn how to marshall all of your resources—your training, education, experience, interests, and personnel—into a formidable marketing tool, tailored to your plan.

You will discover that implementing a quality program in your office will make you and everyone else who works there more productive and happier.

You will become a more active participant in community affairs.

You will adopt new ways to deal with your clients that will make them clients for life.

You will find ways to make your telephone, your business card, your billings, your voice mail, your leisure time, your acquaintances, your successes, your secretary and paralegal, court reporters, the public library, PBS, your waiting room, high schools, even your desk calendar, tools for meeting your marketing plan goals.

You will become a "builder," as William C. Waddell says in *Overcoming Murphy's Law* (AMACOM), of your firm's intangible assets: its knowledge; the confidence and trust it not only enjoys but has in others as well; its commitment to its purpose or ideal; its efficiency; its flexibility and creative sense; its shared attitude of teamwork; and its image in the community, however broad that community might be.

You will, in short, embark on a new course of self- and firm-improvement that will be with you for the rest of your life.

And you will find something else. You will find that by following your plan, you will become a better practitioner.

Chapter One

What Is Marketing for a Small Law Firm or Sole Practitioner?

THE PERCEPTION OF QUALITY

Quality is not measured by me. It's not even measured by you. Quality is in the eyes of the customer.

John Guerra, *AT&T*

The law firm's two-color, half-page ads in the Yellow Pages proclaiming that it specializes in certain areas of practice, classifieds in the evening paper offering divorces for $89.95, and those television ads, dominated by a father figure who thoughtfully removes his glasses at just the right moment, to reassure the audience that, "We care about you, and there's never a charge for the initial consultation": these constitute an image that many people hold of law firm marketing.

To be sure, such ads are marketing tools, and they are sometimes effective in gaining certain types of clients. But they are not the sum and substance of marketing.

Effective marketing is more than the selling of legal services. *It is the creation and preservation of a perception of quality in the mind of the client, a perception that is unique to each client.*

How that perception is created and maintained depends on the needs and desires of each client, yet law firm marketing efforts will generally focus on a number of areas to accomplish the goals of a marketing plan:

1. The creation and implementation of a public and community relations program with definite long- and short-term goals, designed to attract and retain clients.

1

2. The institution of a total quality management system in the office that involves training, education, and client-focused programs.

3. Marketing and advertising programs that conform to state and ABA guidelines and portray a desirable image.

4. Systems to track, measure, and evaluate marketing efforts and provide a basis for correcting and changing when appropriate.

The perception of quality, of course, is sufficient to attract the client, but it is the reality of quality, and the reality of performance, that retains the client.

PERFORMANCE IS REALITY

No one ever excused himself to success.

David Del Dotto

Harold Geneen, the phenomenally successful CEO of ITT (now retired), says that, "It is an immutable law in business that words are words, explanations are explanations, promises are promises—but only performance is reality."

In his book, simply titled *Managing* (Doubleday & Co.), Geneen explains that all the theories of management and leadership—Theory X, Theory Y, and Theory Z, for example—are meaningless without performance. Indeed, his "Theory G" states that "You cannot run a business, or anything else, on a theory."

"Performance alone," he says, "is the best measure of your confidence, competence, and courage. Only performance gives you the freedom to grow as yourself."

His definition of a successful leader in business is, predictably, one who turns in the performance. "No alibis to others or to one's self."

Performance and Geneen are not strangers. During his tenure at ITT, the firm increased its earnings over the previous year for 58 consecutive quarters. No other corporation in American history has been able to accomplish that task.

His business philosophy is contained in what he calls "A Three Sentence Course on Business Management:"

You read a book from beginning to end. You run a business the opposite way. You start with the end, and then you do everything you must to reach it.

His method for leading others to performance can be emulated at all levels of management. By predetermining the desired outcome and expecting your team to "stretch beyond the ordinary, even beyond what they think are their capabilities," to make that outcome a reality, goals—performance—will be met.

It is the responsibility of the leader, Geneen says, "to set the goals. It is his responsibility to point his people in the direction of the goalposts, and tell them how to get there. He is the only person who can do it."

Geneen does not believe that *ordering* people to meet goals made ITT a success. "We were telling them that we were all going to do it together, that [everyone] was there to help them achieve these goals. In short, we were in the same boat, sink or survive, and we would all be rowing very hard, but in the end it would prove to be worthwhile for all of us."

Geneen's brand of leadership—teamwork without pretension, with constant focus on common goals and the promise of mutual reward when the task is completed—is what evokes extraordinary performance from ordinary people.

"Many people," says Geneen, "have asked me from time to time for the secret of my success in business. Usually I avoided giving any answer. Now I can reveal it: The secret of how to succeed in business or in life is that there is no secret. No secret at all. No formula. No theory." Just performance.

Geneen's theory of management is equally applicable to the legal profession. The client will ultimately judge the lawyer not by what he or she says will be accomplished, but by what in fact is accomplished. And the effectiveness of the lawyer's team, partners and associates as well as clerical and paraprofessional staff members, will be in direct proportion to that lawyer's ability to lead them to the successful accomplishment of their goals.

Yet it must be remembered that the ultimate value of what is accomplished will be judged through the eyes of the client and not through the eyes of the lawyer. A good result obtained on behalf of a client may be seen by the client as excellent or as poor, depending upon his or her point of view.

I once had the occasion to represent a young woman in a medical malpractice case where liability was not only not an issue, it was freely admitted by the physician who instructed his liability carrier to settle the matter as rapidly as possible.

The woman, whose breast cancer was allowed to spread by the simple failure to check a lab report, had less than a year to live. She wanted to settle for $100,000, without delay, so she could fulfill a lifelong dream: to travel the world with her husband and two small children. I advised her of the potential value of the case, but she stuck to her wishes, and her husband supported her decision.

The matter was resolved within a matter of weeks, to her satisfaction. Other lawyers criticized me for settling the case for so little, but what mattered was that I met her expectations of quality and performance.

DOES QUALITY WORK ON A SMALL SCALE?

When Roger Telschow hired his first employee 14 years ago, he insisted on being called "Mr. Telschow," and never ate lunch with him. As his printing company grew, he managed by "issuing ultimatums," he says in *Nation's Business.*

"Whenever I used to hear the phrases 'total quality management' or 'zero defects,'" he says, "I would envision sleek, high-tech manufacturing plants with perfect employees, perfect managers, and the latest in machinery and software."

Telschow never imagined that the techniques he read about could apply to Ecoprint, so-called because his firm prides itself on "the most environmentally responsible printing anywhere."

It all changed, however, when he saw that his methods weren't working and asked his employees for help. "I said that I felt as if I had been trying to run the company single-handedly. From now on, I told them, I wanted them to manage their own jobs themselves, but I would help in any way I could. The bottom line, I said, is that to succeed, we've got to work together. And, I added, just call me Roger."

The improvement was immediate. Telschow recognized that the newly empowered employees seemed to have an investment in the firm's success. New ideas flowed from them to reduce errors and speed production. And Telschow found that he had more time to train and become involved in increasing productivity.

Telschow soon found that "we were working as a team, guided by a strong desire to satisfy the customer."

The teamwork paid off. In 1991, Ecoprint became the first small business ever to win a coveted US Senate Productivity Award. Customer satisfaction is over 95 percent; more than 99 percent of all orders are delivered on the day promised; absenteeism is down to an average of one day per year per employee; and his employees outproduce the industry average by 57 percent.

"We learned a lot on our way to that award," he says. "For one thing, a small business can manage by using total quality methods even if the firm doesn't call them TQM.

"The important thing to remember," says Telschow, "is that it is people—not robots—that make a quality program work. You can even call them by their first names and still get results."

That you are a sole practitioner or a partner in a small firm does not mean that quality programs will not work for you. If anything, you may need them even more than the large firm with a multitude of clients to fall back on, if only one client leaves.

STARTING AT THE END BY SETTING GOALS

Success isn't making a better mousetrap or even a million dollars. Success is much more personal than that. It's meeting the goals you set for yourself.

Me

Taking Geneen's advice to heart, the beginning of any marketing plan is the visualization of what it is to achieve. Only with the ends in mind can goals be set to meet that end.

After an Olympic swimming competition, a young woman on the US team who had failed to win a medal was smiling, and the reporter asked her why. "I set a personal best time today," she said. "So, I'm happy."

She had a goal to reach, to do her best, and meeting that goal was a reward in itself.

Realistic goals are important to the success of any marketing plan, or any of life's endeavors, for that matter. As a partner or sole practitioner, it is your responsibility to ensure that the goals you set are achievable. Nothing drains morale faster than attempting to meet goals that are outside your office's ability.

How do you set goals that enhance job performance, motivate both you and the members of your firm, and provide true job satisfaction when they are met? Here are some ideas that work.

- Involve each member of your firm—professional, paraprofessional, and clerical—in setting goals. Input from people with varied skills and experience may save a goal from certain failure. It also makes everyone feel more involved and committed to the outcome, which translates into job satisfaction later when the goal is achieved.

- Define the problem. In *Successful Management by Objectives,* Karl Albrecht writes that this is a "fuzzy," not a concrete goal, but finding out what needs to be fixed is the first step. "Our billable hours are falling off" is an example of a fuzzy that will later become a goal.

- State what the desired payoff will be if the problem is solved. Having a payoff gives each team member a reason to work toward solving the problem, whether it is a bonus, recognition, or simply a sense of accomplishment. "If the number of billable hours improves, we'll be the most successful firm in the county again."

- Spell out the conditions that must be met to make sure the payoff occurs. For example: "We have to get two more hospitals as clients by January 1." *Note that the goal now set is concrete* and spells out exactly what must happen and by when. Success can be measured by whether the goal is met by a specific deadline and progress toward achieving that goal can likewise be monitored.

- List the actions that have to be taken to make sure the conditions are met: "Each of us has to bring in two new clients each month with an average of five billable hours each week." "We have to improve our customer relations so we don't lose the Acme account." "We have to get together with the people who maintain our computers and have them correct the problem on our billing program that our clients are complaining about."

- Select the best actions listed and make a plan that will ensure that the goal is reached.

- And then, as Robert B. Maddux writes in *Team Building,* follow the progress of the work, reinforce achievement, and assist in problem solving. Be a "challenger, prober, coach, and enabler." Be prepared to modify the plan along the way to compensate for unforeseen occurrences like changes in the economy or unsuspected competition. And follow through when the goal is met by ensuring that the payoff is realized.

Meeting a goal can be its own reward and it will strengthen your firm by encouraging cooperative problem solving while still allowing individual members to "set their personal bests," as did the young Olympic swimmer.

KEEPING THE CLIENT FIRST

Consistent, high-quality service boils down to two equally important things: caring and competence.

Chip R. Bell and Ron Zemke, *Service Wisdom*

There is a decidedly human tendency to keep the welfare of the firm, and ourselves, of paramount interest in the creation of a marketing plan. We tend, that is, to look at what we will gain for ourselves rather than for our clients. If the installation of a new on-line research computer system will save time for lawyers and paralegals, do we pass on that savings to the client? If we become more productive, do we use our new skills and abilities to make our clients more productive?

In industry, managers have only recently learned that only by putting the needs of their customers first will they become more competitive and, hence, more profitable. Law firms must also acknowledge that their worth, in their clients' eyes, consists not so much in what they can do for a client, but in the value they add to their client's business. How does what the lawyer does make the client more productive, more cost-effective, more able to compete in its marketplace? For the plaintiff's attorney, the question is, in what way does the lawyer shape the expectations of the client and then meet those expectations?

By studying the needs of present clients and those the firm wishes to target as potential clients, lawyers can develop their practices and abilities to meet those needs. How do you discover what your clients' needs are?

To provide your clients with the service and quality they want, you must ask and listen.

That's what Digital Equipment Corporation does, and the result is a customer-oriented service system that keeps the customer happy.

The hallmark of the system is a "one call" program in effect at its 14 Customer Service Centers (CSCs) nationwide. Troubleshooters trained to diagnose and correct problems with the computer company's hard- and software make sure that when a customer calls, the problem is solved or a team is sent to fix it with just one call. If the problem can be corrected over the phone, there is never a charge. By listening, the technicians gain valuable information as to what improvements need to be made.

Working 24 hours a day, the CSCs provide support whenever the customer requires it, not when it's convenient to Digital Equipment

Corporation (DEC). That's something the customers have told the company they wanted in response to annual field surveys.

Customers actually have helped make DEC a leader in the business and personal computer market. According to an article in *Fortune* magazine, DEC builds its computers to customers' specifications rather than "trying to predict their equipment needs from a planning committee. That puts a lot of responsibility on the lower-level staff. They must know what the customers want, and communicate it to the design team."

But higher-level staff don't just sit in their offices. It's common for senior executives to roll up their sleeves and spend a day in the warehouse, getting to understand the problems of filling orders firsthand. By being involved in every aspect of the operations of the company, they can better plan to meet the customers' problems.

When customers complained, for example, that salesmen weren't spending enough time with them, DEC placed the salesmen on straight salary, eliminating the pressure to make sales instead of making customers. The payoff is obvious: the salesmen are free to spend more time helping their customers and understanding their needs. The customers are more satisfied, and the salesmen become more familiar with their needs.

By listening, understanding, and responding to their customers' needs, law firms, too, can create not only new ways to solve problems, but new services to meet their clients' needs as well. As Tom Peters says in *Thriving on Chaos* (Alfred A. Knopf), "Listening to customers must become everyone's business. With most competitors moving ever faster, the race will go to those who listen most intently."

To help the people in your firm become better listeners, reward service accomplishments the way you would reward someone who brought in a coveted client. Recognize those who take the extra time to help a client and empower them to ask clients in which ways they and your firm's service can be improved. Then take the necessary steps to fulfill the clients' expectations.

And, according to Tim Lawler, who owns the Milwaukee franchise of Management Recruiters International, Inc., you can retain your best clients by keeping the following points in mind:

- Share your knowledge with your clients and educate them with seminars or talks about the services you can provide.

- Listen to what they say about you and your competition, and give them what they want, not what you want them to want.

- Stand by your guarantees, no matter what. Let them know that your commitment to client satisfaction is backed by performance.
- Help clients make informed decisions, even if it means no billable hours for a particular matter. They'll remember that you placed their welfare above your own.
- Keep in touch with your clients. If you see something that might interest them, even if it's not related to the services you can provide, write them a note or give them a call. And don't bill them for your time in keeping them informed.
- Hold a client-appreciation day. Invite them for coffee and doughnuts. Have a tailgate party at the stadium, or a dinner cruise. Make them feel wanted, and appreciated.
- Follow up the conclusion of each matter with a call to make sure your client is satisfied.

ARE YOU CLIENT-FOCUSED?

To find out whether you and the others with whom you work are putting the client first on a day-to-day basis, take the self-evaluation quiz on the next page. You may photocopy the quiz for use by others, lawyers, paralegals, clerical, and support staff, in your firm. Completing this exercise will help all of you redirect your efforts. Simply circle the appropriate response.

Putting the customer first is more than a slogan, it means placing the customer's needs ahead of your own. If you marked any questions No or Need Improvement, you already know where you need help in making your customer-first program succeed.

It's a Team Thing, Too

There is no place in an organization for the overly ambitious person who only looks out for number one. The best way to channel your ambition is to be ambitious—not for yourself—but for your organization. Put all your energies into accomplishing team goals first. After that, all the other things, like your recognition and advancement, will take care of themselves.

F. A. Manske, *Secrets of Effective Leadership*
(Leadership Education and Development, Inc.)

In order for the small law firm or sole practitioner to compete with larger firms for the same or similar clients, it is crucial that every person on the

	Yes	*No*	*Need Improvement*
1. Do you meet with your clients more than twice a year and ask them how you could improve your service?			
2. When a client complains, do you do what you can to rectify the situation, rather than make excuses?			
3. Do you know how much revenue your firm receives from each client?			
4. Have you taken the time to tour your client's plant or store, in an effort to learn more about his or her business?			
5. Do you make "How Can We Improve Service?" a regular topic of discussion at firm meetings?			
6. Have you ever invited a client to visit your offices?			
7. When changes are proposed, do you request the opportunity to discuss with your clients how the changes will affect them?			
8. Do you look for ways in which to save your clients money?			
9. Have you ever used any of your own services, to see how your clients view them?			
10. Do you try to solve your clients' problems with just one phone call?			

lawyer's team—each partner, associate, paraprofessional, and secretary, even the people hired as messengers, process servers, expert witnesses, and court reporters—contribute to the success of the marketing plan by making a commitment to the quality of service rendered to the client, as well as to the impression of professionalism that the lawyer or firm wants to portray in the community.

To accomplish this, the lawyer or firm must make a commitment to building a team that has excellence as its primary goal: excellence in client relations, excellence in research, excellence in the drafting of documents, excellence in the way the telephone is answered, excellence in the preparation of error-free billings, excellence in all things.

"Building is the heart of the manager's job," says William C. Waddell in his book, *Overcoming Murphy's Law* (AMACOM). "It means increasing the assets of the firm. For most managers, more often than not, the opportunity for building lies with the intangible assets rather than with the tangible."

According to Waddell, there are nine areas in which a leader should strive to build values and qualities.

1. *Knowledge.* Waddell says that knowledge of human behavior, management principles, your industry, and of business generally, is the most important asset a firm has. Encourage yourself and your coworkers to grow in these areas.

2. *Confidence and trust.* "Building confidence and trust is more than a two-way street," Waddell says. "You need to work on the relationships in all directions, up, down, and sideways. Confidence and trust are needed in all transactions and relationships."

3. *Responsibility.* Responsibility means commitment to the organization's ideal or purpose. To illustrate the point, Waddell recalls the story of the three stonecutters. In response to the question, "What are you doing for a living," the first replies, "I am doing a fair day's work." The second answers, "I am cutting the best stones that can be cut." And the third, who has a clear sense of his responsibility, proclaims, "I am building a cathedral."

4. *Effectiveness.* Make sure coworkers understand the goals and their priorities to be effective at their jobs. They must also keep in mind that doing the job right is more important than doing it quickly.

5. *Efficiency.* Allow workers a hand in designing and improving the way in which they approach their jobs. Always be open to suggestions for improving efficiency.

6. *Team organization.* "Teamwork in all endeavors calls for a dedication to common goals and cooperative effort to meet those goals," says Waddell. The leader's task is to constantly strive to build a team in which individual goals are subordinate to those of the team.

7. *Flexibility and creativity.* Leaders must create an atmosphere in which change is acceptable and in which people are permitted to fail. View mistakes as opportunities for learning, and suggestions as the bases for improvement.

8. *External relations.* Goodwill, developed in the community, speaks well not only of your team, but of your organization. External relations can also be the source of information about your market, your competition, and developments in your industry.

9. *Winning attitude.* Set high standards for yourself and your team and meet them. When faced with seemingly insurmountable obstacles, take strenuous steps to overcome them. Winning is a mind-set that can be learned and cultivated. Better yet, it can be habit forming.

Waddell says that leaders should make being a builder and a winner a part of their self-image. "Treat success as the normal condition," he says, and build for it in the future.

GET YOUR TEAM TO ACT LIKE OWNERS

If you are not contributing to the solution of the problem, then you are part of the problem yourself.

Chinese Proverb

Teams that think and act as though they own the firm are more dedicated and productive than those who simply punch the clock and wait for payday.

According to Roger Fritz, "Getting your employees to think and act like owners is the single greatest factor in your company's long-term success.

"When employees think like owners, their whole outlook changes. They put more effort in their work. They quibble less about hours and working conditions. They want more information about sales and profits. They become concerned about the company's future. They ask more penetrating questions, seek background information, and want explanations for decisions that are made."

In short, they care about the organization and their roles in it. As the leader of your team, it's up to you to help them develop an ownership attitude, and Fritz has the plan to make that work.

In an article for *Entrepreneur,* Fritz states that helping your team develop that attitude involves two basic steps: "You knowing your employees' goals, and your employees knowing your goals. If your employees believe you truly care about their objectives, they will care about yours."

Fritz suggests that leaders look at the problem in the form of two questions: What do they want? What do you want?

Your team members probably want the same things that most employees want, says Fritz. Beyond income-related benefits and satisfactory wages, they want trust.

Trust is a two-way street. They want to trust you and they want to be trusted by you. "If your employees trust you, they will give you the benefit of the doubt when you want to make changes in production, services, or schedules," says Fritz. "If they don't trust you, they will always suspect that changes may benefit the company (or even you personally), but rarely help them."

What you want, of course, is for your team to meet its goals. You can do that, says Fritz, by letting them know what your short- and long-term goals are. "If your employees are going to think like business owners, they have to know how a business owner thinks. This means you!"

He advises leaders to take their team members into their confidence, treat them like insiders, important members of the team. And let them know how they stand to benefit from helping you meet the goals you have set.

"Once you let your staff into your confidence, your goals will become their goals, and your employees will work doubly hard to reach them. And as your company meets its objectives, you'll fulfill your employees' goals," he concludes.

EVERY TEAM NEEDS A LEADER—AND THAT MEANS YOU

Managers do things right. Leaders do the right thing.

Anonymous

For your marketing plan to work, and for your team to succeed, there needs to be a leader—one who can meld the individual strengths of everyone on staff into a dedicated force that is eager, able, trained, and ready to meet the goals that you and they set together. That leader is you, and you must sharpen or acquire the skills necessary to assume that role.

There are myriad volumes written on what traits good leaders have, whether they are born or made, and how to become one. In reality, all such guidance boils down to one simple truth: good leaders get others to do what is necessary for the good of the group, not by coercion, but by setting the example, and by teaching.

There are no secrets of being a great leader or teacher, but great leaders and teachers do have many of the same qualities according to Jack H. Grossman, associate professor of management at Chicago's De Paul University.

"Techniques for managing people that do not come from the soul come across as phony and artificial," Grossman says in a *Chicago Tribune* editorial. "Unless managers' people-managing techniques are extensions of their values and beliefs, they will, almost invariably, fail."

Extraordinary leaders, Grossman discovered as a result of a survey he conducted, try to bring out the best in the people to whom they are responsible. And, more often than not, they have the following 10 traits that they share with great teachers:

- They really listen. Grossman calls listening the "single" most important way of demonstrating genuine caring. They "read between the lines" to sense things that words alone cannot convey, such as body language and facial expressions.

- They are interested in the people who report to them not just as employees, but as people as well. They genuinely care about their coworkers.

- They clearly express the expectations they have of others. They let others know that they have faith in their abilities to accomplish a given task and give them the freedom to get it done.

- They are eager to share knowledge, to explain, and to answer questions without making the inquirer feel inferior.

- They reinforce positive behaviors by complimenting good work and discourage poor performances by offering constructive criticism.

- They can be trusted to keep their word and to not make promises they will be unable to keep. As Grossman says, "They consider their word as binding as a legal contract because it violates their sense of propriety—their values—to deliberately disappoint people they genuinely care about."

- They are flexible and open to new ideas. They will admit mistakes and alter their plans when circumstances warrant.

- They are enthusiastic and have a good sense of humor that is infectious and helps to increase productivity.

- They set standards and goals that challenge others to strive to do their best.

- They are in control, and their confidence in themselves inspires others to have confidence in them. "From the employee's standpoint," Grossman says, "it's like being in the constant presence of a commercial airline pilot who, the moment he welcomes the passengers, says in effect, 'Lean back, relax, I'll get you to your destination because you're in the hands of a true professional.'"

Grossman believes that those who aspire to management positions should learn "the art of good teaching" from those who have a reputation as outstanding managers, because the art probably comes naturally to them.

It is the honest concern for the welfare of others that sets extraordinary leaders apart from those who merely manage people.

A wise leader not only recognizes that his or her team members have lives outside the workplace, but gains their loyalty and trust by making accommodations for their personal demands as well.

According to Lorraine Calvacca in *Working Woman* magazine, Marilynn Davis, vice president of the risk-financing division at American Express, is able to strike a true balance between work and the personal concerns of the eight-member team she heads.

"People are your biggest component," says Davis. "You can't expect them to be machines."

Mike Rubenstein, director of risk finance, relates the following anecdote about Davis's winning leadership style: He and Davis had to agree on a date for a major presentation they were to give to a corporate financial officer who had suggested October 31 as an option. Davis ruled it out, says Rubenstein, because she "knew I had a young son and that it was important to me to see him in his dinosaur Halloween costume."

The presentation was not jeopardized by the selection of an alternate date, and Davis' concern for the personal happiness of her team member had its own reward. According to Rubenstein, the way Davis strikes a balance between work and personal concerns "makes life much more interesting and fun."

Davis also "shows her concern through inquiries about employees' families and acknowledgements of watersheds such as weddings and graduations," says Calvacca, who concludes that "Davis builds team spirit and morale by tempering business with pleasure."

When making long-term plans, ask at team meetings whether dates being proposed would conflict with members' personal plans for vacations, family reunions, and similar affairs. If possible, rearrange plans to accommodate matters of particular importance. Then make a note in your calendar of those special days and follow up with a handwritten note wishing them a good time.

Taking the time to demonstrate that what they do outside the workplace is important to you, too, will pay off on the job in terms of productivity.

Demanding excellence and showing personal concern for the members of your team need not be conflicting goals, however.

Ultimately, your effectiveness as a leader is measured by your ability to demand and get excellence from your team.

"The key as a leader is to demand excellence for *their* sake, not just yours or the organization's," say Jimmy Calano and Jeff Salzman in their book, *Career Tracking* (Simon & Schuster). Here's what they recommend to accomplish that goal:

1. Don't let the importance of emphasizing positive reinforcement downplay the need for toughness and discipline. "To see someone doing something wrong and not correct the mistake is just another way of showing you don't care," Calano and Salzman say. "Most people are inspired by knowing that their leader believes in their excellence and won't accept anything less from them."

2. Spotlight one area of improvement at a time. Give your team members immediate feedback, positive and negative. "People need to know how they're doing *now.*"

3. Show them you're serious about improvement. Calano and Salzman recommend you dramatize the importance you place on improvement by conducting a reverse performance evaluation. "It reinforces their perception of you as a leader open to criticism and improvement," they say.

"When you hand out the forms, be sure to ask for specific examples to back up vague praise or criticism. This form—and your follow-through—will open wide the lines of communications." Let your team members know that you will accept their appraisals in an open-minded spirit and will work on areas they see a need for you to improve.

The authors recommend that this reverse performance appraisal be repeated every six months or so, and, if you receive a too-good-to-be-true review, send it back with a note saying, "Thanks, but nobody's *this* perfect. Surely I need to improve somewhere. Try again."

If the glowing report comes back, congratulate yourself, say Calano and Salzman. "You're on your way to being the boss everyone wants to work with."

WHAT KIND OF A LEADER ARE YOU?

The purpose of the following interactive exercise is to give you some idea of your ability as a leader in your firm, as well as to give you an indication of the areas in which improvements can be made.

Good leaders are always concerned with self-improvement. They constantly seek new and better ways to get their jobs done and seek to hone old skills that need to be sharpened. Simply place a check mark on the appropriate line to the right of each question.

	Yes	*No*
1. Do you consistently recognize employees for a job well done?		
2. Do you have true concern for the welfare of the people who work for you?		
3. Do you solicit new ideas from your coworkers?		
4. Do you delegate responsibility (without micro-managing projects)?		
5. Do you act quickly on employee complaints?		
6. Do you discipline fairly and effectively?		
7. Do you discuss work assignments with employees to gain their insight and involvement?		
8. Do you practice fairness, not favoritism?		
9. Do you stress results more than methods, so employees are free to use their creativity?		
10. Do you sit in your office, or do you get out and talk to the people who work with you?		
11. Do you ask all members—not just fellow lawyers—how *you* could improve?		
12. Do you encourage the free exchange of ideas?		
13. Do you set a good example?		

If answering any of these questions made you feel a little uncomfortable or left you wondering whether you could improve in that area, then you should concentrate on those areas for self-improvement.

STAFF TRAINING

One of the most important jobs the lawyer in a small firm or a sole practitioner has is also one of the most neglected: the training of those who work in the office and who have client contact, directly or indirectly, whether they answer the phone, type the letters, prepare the billings, schedule depositions, or conduct initial interviews. Each and every one of them should have a business card that reads: "Jan Doe, Smith & Jones, Client Relations Specialist," because that is not just a function of his or her job, it is the only job he or she has.

It is not enough to train the lawyers, paraprofessionals, and clerical staff to do their jobs competently, though that must be done. They must be trained to understand that the way in which they accomplish their assigned tasks has a direct bearing on the success or failure of the firm as a whole.

A former chairman of a large computer manufacturing company was once asked who the most important individual in his organization was. Without hesitation, he replied that it was the guy on the loading dock who made sure that the boxes of computers were safely placed in the trucks. If that individual failed to do his job right, if he dropped a box and smashed the computer inside, the customer would never know, or care, about the quality safeguards inside the plant, or the excellence of manufacturing of the components shipped to him. His sole contact with the company would be a broken and useless piece of equipment.

The same can be said of a law firm. It doesn't matter if the lawyers who work there are the most able in their fields. If a potential client calls and is put on interminable hold, or if a letter sent has misspellings and mounds of white-out, or if the waiting room is dirty and unkempt, or any other negative impression is given, that is the only impression the potential client has of your firm's ability to help with his or her problems. And it will be a lasting impression, one that he or she will share with others.

Call your office from the road and listen to how the phone is answered. "Law Offices," is a common greeting. But whose law offices? What is the tone of voice that the answering party uses? Is there background noise— laughter, for example—that detracts from the impression you want to give callers? If you are put on hold, is there an apology for keeping you waiting? If you have voice mail, does it perturb you to be switched from nonhuman to nonhuman too many times? Are your telephones used productively?

If you think that you and your staff already know how to use a telephone, you should read Madeline Bodin's book, *Using the Telephone More Effectively* (Barron's Educational Series). In it, she explains how you can better utilize the most important piece of business equipment you have to save time and money, and to make your calls more productive.

Cutting the amount of time you spend on the phone leaves time for other projects. Bodin suggests the following ways to cut the time spent on the phone:

Have people use your facsimile machine to deliver one-way information such as statistics or meeting dates. It is less time-consuming and more accurate than transcribing figures over the phone.

Before you make a call, write down an agenda—the points you want to make with the other party—and stick to it. It's easy to get sidetracked during a telephone conversation and forget the reason you called. Prepare for important calls the way you would prepare for a meeting.

Save socializing—"How's your golf game"—for the end of the conversation, after the business is conducted. Then, if one of the parties is forced to cut the call short, all that is eliminated is chitchat.

If you call one person several times during the course of a business day, save up a few short calls and make one, longer one. The person you call will appreciate not being interrupted as frequently.

Make sure your secretary or assistant has a list of VIPs, such as major customers or suppliers, whose phone calls you should take even if you're in a meeting.

And, if you connect with voice mail, use it to your advantage. Use the system to leave a terse message that gets your point across. Having a prewritten script helps.

Bodin also has a solution to the game of telephone tag:

"When leaving a message, think of it as setting a tentative appointment. Ask what time the person who called is expected to be available, and say you will call back at that time. When you leave a message for the person to call you, leave a specific day and time when you will be at your desk to receive the call."

According to Bodin, the telephone can be a painful interruption in your business or a vital and effective tool for getting things done. It all depends on how effectively you use it.

Training your staff and yourself to be more productive and client-focused in the routines of daily tasks is a critical task, and one that should not be ignored. But it is one that can be done with a minimum of effort on your part, if you use "benchmarking" to help you improve staff performance.

Benchmarking is nothing more than identifying the best provider of a particular service or product, meeting with them to see how they achieve their standard of excellence, and then adopting their methods for your firm. In grade school, they called it copying another's work. But in business, it's an acceptable way to improve performance rapidly and inexpensively.

If there are professional service providers—accountants, doctors, other law firms—whose services and institutional attitudes you find to be better than those offered by your office, find out how they do it and adapt their techniques to your organization.

Similarly, make note of the way in which others provide services poorly and tell your staff what was done that you found unprofessional. Norman Schwartzkopf once said that he learned more about leadership from officers who were horrible examples than those who were good leaders, because he learned how *not* to do the job.

BECOME INVOLVED IN YOUR COMMUNITY

There is no more potent form of advertising than the sincere recommendation of someone who has nothing to gain by doing so. By being involved in your community you and your firm will generate goodwill that money cannot buy, and you will also realize that doing good works makes you feel good.

Make a commitment to charities in your community, too. Studies have shown that companies that make a habit of donating money to community programs or charities generate goodwill and also enjoy higher employee morale. Surprisingly, small companies generally give more per employee to community service programs than do larger firms, according to the US Small Business Administration.

The Council on Foundations has published two books to help small organizations develop effective programs for giving. Each costs $12 and can be obtained through the Council of Foundations by writing to its Publications Department at 1828 L Street, N.W., Washington, D.C. 20036.

Developing Small Corporate Giving Programs, by Lisa Berger, gives practical information on how to form the most effective program. Included are guidelines that a firm can use in deciding whether to give to an organization, plus a sample mission statement for a firm's contributions program.

Effective Roles for Small Corporate Giving Programs, by Paul Ylvisaker, provides 20 strategies for enhancing your company's program to "do more with less." The author suggests, for example, that a firm can help nonprofit organizations not just with contributions but also by lending office space and employees' time and expertise for specific projects.

And make pro bono work a requirement for yourself and the other lawyers in your office. Volunteer to be a guardian ad litem for abused children, or represent the indigent as passionately as you would a paying client. It will remind you of what being a lawyer is all about: helping people.

WHAT DOES ALL THIS HAVE TO DO WITH MARKETING LEGAL SERVICES?

Teamwork, focusing on what your clients want and need, involvement in community affairs, leadership, setting realistic goals, empowering people on your staff to unleash their creativity and become the most productive employees they can be, instilling in everyone who works with, and for you, the belief that client relations is, first, last, and always, their only job, learning to listen and become more caring while still demanding and getting excellence from your staff, being receptive to new ideas—wherever they originate—and developing the ability to adapt and change plans to accommodate changes in your firm, your clients' business and/or personal milieu, and the world at large, constantly seeking improvement toward the elusive goal of excellence. What do these have to do with marketing legal services?

Everything!

Before you can market excellence, you must begin to seek it in every aspect of your practice. Through training of your staff, continuing education, forgetting self for client and employee, doing what is right rather than what is expedient, and devoting your time and effort to being the best counsellor you can be in whatever field of law you practice, you will be able to achieve excellence.

And that is the most effective marketing tool you can have.

Chapter Two

The Elements of a Marketing Plan

WHY PLAN?

According to a 1993 survey conducted by the National Association of Legal Vendors, the financial outlook for law firms was again bleak. One-third of the firms surveyed indicated that their revenues fell short of their predictions in 1992. Fewer than half expected partners' incomes to increase. More than half said they would hire no new associates, 75 percent said they would add no new partners, and 80 percent indicated they would make no additions to their support staff.

Because of the competition for clients and need for enhanced lawyer productivity, however, 41 percent said they would be increasing expenditures for marketing and business development, and 52 percent indicated they would be spending more on computers and automation.

Business development is now not a luxury for firms that want to remain competitive, it is a necessity, and developing a marketing plan is critical for survival, not just prosperity. Corporate clients who once obeyed the dictates of firms whose partners charged as much as $400 an hour are now calling the shots, demanding to see all court filings, slashing bills, requiring cost estimates and detailed plans, picking cost-effective firms, saying no to more than one lawyer at a deposition. They are changing the way big firms practice law.

As a result, law firms in the early 90s were firing associates or asking them to accept salary freezes, paying more attention to their clients' business needs, learning how to read spreadsheets and make forecasts, and hiring marketing professionals and total quality management gurus like Robert H. Waterman, Jr. (coauthor of *In Search of Excellence*) to help them develop and implement their plans.

The impact on small firms and sole practitioners has not been so dramatic; their clients are smaller. But the effect on those "lower on the food chain" will trickle down as medium-sized firms intensify their marketing efforts in competition for the work that remains after the big fish are finished eating.

Small firms and sole practitioners have another, more compelling problem to contend with, too. As the larger firms become more streamlined and less dependent upon associates' billable hours to pay partners' salaries and perks, and thus hire fewer associates, there will be more lawyers entering the legal marketplace as sole practitioners and a greater number of small firms.

The American Bar Association estimates that by the year 2000 there will be one million lawyers in the United States, an increase of 240,000 from 1990, each one struggling for the same client base.

THE BENEFITS OF PLANNING

Just as the mere establishment of goals is an effective motivational and organizational tool, the act of planning has benefits, too. As Dwight D. Eisenhower once said, "Plans are nothing. Planning is everything."

What Eisenhower meant was that planning a framework for action, not a rigid, immutable set of rules that can never be violated, prepares the planner to meet challenges, both anticipated and unanticipated. To be effective, plans must be amenable to change. Rarely will a plan remain pristine throughout its life.

And through planning, you and the others in your office will gain a greater understanding of your individual strengths and weaknesses, the areas in which your practice is profitable and where waste and losses can be curtailed, what you can and should do to help your firm grow its assets. You will also learn what does and doesn't work for your firm, for your clients, for your community. And, you will gain the ability to react to events in a positive manner, because the goal of your plan will be there as a polestar to guide your activities no matter what obstacles are thrown before you.

DETERMINE YOUR OBJECTIVE

It is axiomatic that determining your objectives, that is, setting the ultimate goals of your marketing plan, is the most important aspect of your plan.

In Chapter One, the elements of a successful goal were discussed, but they should be reiterated here.

- The goal should be clear, understood by everyone on staff.
- It should have a deadline, allowing coordination of other matters and ensuring that it is accomplished and not forgotten.
- The goal should be measurable, so that its success or failure can be judged.
- It should meet a demand in your marketplace.
- And, the goal should be attainable.

ASSESS YOUR STRENGTHS AND WEAKNESSES

To be attainable, you and your staff must either now possess the ability to accomplish that goal, or you must take steps to acquire that ability through education, affiliation with others, or the hiring of additional staff who already possess the required skills.

To determine whether your skills are up to the task, you and your staff must frankly appraise each others' strengths and weaknesses. This is not an exercise for those who have easily bruised egos, but it is a necessary exercise. It is called a skill inventory.

Here's how it's done:

1. Determine what your desired goal is.

2. Ask yourself what skills one must have to attain that goal. If you aren't sure what skill set is necessary, develop a friendship with someone who is successful in the area and emulate the skills he or she has. And don't limit yourself to technical skills, or those unique to the legal profession. Consider generic skills as well, such as the acquisition of public speaking skills, salesmanship, the ability to write business letters or interpret business plans, or the ability to read and understand a hospital chart.

3. Ask others you trust to tell you, frankly, whether you have the requisite skills. Ask them to rate your skills on a scale from 1 to 10 in each area, with 10 being perfect.

4. Without looking at the ratings others have given you, rate yourself in the same areas, using the same scale.

5. Compare the ratings to see if you and the others agree on your skills. If the ratings agree, you will have a fair idea of the areas in which improvement is called for. If they do not agree, err on the side of caution

and give credence to how the others rated you. It is how others perceive your skills that is ultimately important.

6. Discover ways in which you can improve those skills or, if necessary, obtain those skills for your practice by hiring others.

7. Set goals for self-improvement, if appropriate. Again, these should be concrete goals with deadlines and ways to measure performance. Don't say that you will take a trial practice course. Make a commitment to take the July 15 course on trial practice offered by your local bar association.

8. Follow through with your commitment.

9. As a means of measuring whether you are meeting your self-improvement goals, conduct another skill inventory assessment after you have met your goals to determine whether the steps you have taken have had the desired result. If not, go back to step 6.

10. Change your goals as necessary to reflect what can be accomplished.

WHAT SERVICES WILL BE REQUIRED IN THE FUTURE?

Your plan should also reflect the realities for the future of your practice in your locality. If, for example, a manufacturer has made plans to open a facility in your county, you may want to investigate whether you should prepare to offer services that will then be in demand, such as the recognized need for additional providers of workers' compensation representation.

You should also be alert to changes in federal, state, and local laws that will open up new areas of practice: The enactment of the Americans with Disabilities Act, for example, which has spawned more than 3,000 complaints in its first year, still offers an opportunity to provide new and needed representation for both plaintiff and defense attorneys.

Changes in technology bring with them new and exciting legal challenges. When I graduated from law school there were no PCs, let alone a subspecialty of the law that dealt with protecting the intellectual property rights of people who design the programs for them.

If you are in a rural county, where the bar is small, your plan might take into account the areas of practice that will be vacated by lawyers who are approaching retirement age.

In short, any change in the economic or demographic conditions of your practice locale will bring with it opportunities for expansion or change. The successful lawyer will be able to anticipate the needs of the future and plan to meet them adequately.

WHAT COMPETITION DO (WILL) YOU HAVE?

Any business or marketing plan needs to assess the present and future competition for the proposed services. A sole practitioner in a large, northern city would likely have a difficult time establishing herself as a labor lawyer; the competition for clients in that field is fierce among the giant firms. But there might still be room for a sole practitioner in the same city whose practice is limited to representing plaintiffs in perinatal medical malpractice cases or family-owned business bankruptcies, if those niches are not filled.

If there is competition, what will set your firm apart from the pack as better? Why should a client come to your firm rather than to Smith & Jones? What expertise do you have that can be used to market your services better? How does their service or pricing compare to yours?

A plaintiff's attorney who wants to represent the families of victims of aircraft accidents may be as capable as another in product liability law, but if he has a pilot's license, that fact alone may be enough to sway potential clients to choose his services.

WHAT IS THE MARKET FOR YOUR SERVICES?

Whatever services you decide to offer should be directed at some definable segment of the population. The size and geographical distribution of that population will determine how you will disseminate information about those services to the target audience.

By way of example, if you intend to be a general practitioner in a small town, you will likely concentrate your marketing efforts in that community. A lawyer who specializes in admiralty law, however, may see the eastern seaboard as defining the geographic boundaries of her practice, and her clients may be of international scope.

The more specialized the practice, the more diffuse the audience, and the more regional, or even global, your efforts must be to attract clients interested in using your services.

In any event, there must be sufficient market research to determine whether the service is necessary and the size your "community" must be to support your practice.

Market research is a very complex field. You may well be advised to engage the services of a firm skilled in conducting such research before you continue with your plan.

DEVELOP A MARKETING STRATEGY

Once you have set your goals, analyzed your strengths and weaknesses, studied the competition and determined what, and where, your pool of potential clients is, you are ready to develop a strategy that has as its aim convincing them to use you.

How you reach potential clients will be through one or more of the following means:

1. Advertising, through print, direct mail, and electronic media, or a combination of these methods, designed to appeal to the nature and needs of your audience. Advertising also entails the production of brochures, pamphlets, and, in some cases, even the creation of client-focused magazines.

2. Community and public relations efforts, with the size and geographic distribution of your audience determining the size of your community. From sponsoring public relations programs and Little League teams to paying experienced writers with valuable contacts to get your name strategically placed in print or arrange appearances as an expert on talk shows, PR and community relations programs can have a tremendous impact on your market.

3. Client relations improvements, to maintain existing relationships and forge better relationships with future clients. The crux of client relations is training current employees to become client-focused and hiring those who have the ability to market themselves and your firm. This includes all professional, paraprofessional, and clerical employees—anyone who comes into contact with the public.

4. Improving, constantly, the quality of the services you deliver to your client and the cost-effectiveness of those services. According to an article in *Business Week,* the Chicago-based firm of Kirkland & Ellis installed an electronic mail system to link its offices with General Motors, a major client. The system eliminated duplicating, faxing, and overnight

mail costs, which were expenses charged to GM. Thomas A. Gottschalk, the firm's partner in charge of billing, estimates that GM's bills were reduced by as much as one-third.

5. To develop the strategy, you should determine first what the problem area is in which improvement is sought, list the ways in which the problem can be approached by each method, assess the costs of doing each, and make a financial commitment to those approaches, based upon your ability.

[Remember: It doesn't matter whether you can afford to spend $500 or $5,000. It is the act of planning and the commitment to developing the plan that are of greatest importance.]

6. And, as you implement the strategy, continually track the success and failure of each program. Seek excellence in your marketing plan, just as you do in your practice, by changing your strategy to do more of what works and eliminate what does not.

TRACKING SUCCESS AND FAILURE

The easiest way to track your success is to do what large firms, such as Chicago's Winston & Strawn, do. They ask their clients for feedback.

Small firms can also ask clients why they chose their firm and, during and after representation, in what areas they can improve their services.

If your firm has available telephone lines, or can engage the services of an answering service, use separate numbers for certain ads, press releases, or promotions. Callers who use that line will be those who are responding to your efforts. This is particularly useful to track the success of big ticket marketing efforts, such as television advertisements.

Direct mailings can be tracked quite simply by placing a code number on the return envelope that is keyed to the particular mailing.

How each marketing effort is tracked is not as important as the fact that it is tracked in some manner so that its success or failure can be measured and, ultimately, a determination can be made that the cost was worth the effort in terms of new business generated.

THE PLAN

On the following pages, a graphic representation of a sample marketing plan is set forth. Don't fill in the blanks quite yet. But, as you read the remainder of this book, imagine how you might set, and plan to meet, primary and intermediate goals, and visualize how they will all work together to assist you and your firm in meeting the overall goal.

Note that, at the top, there is a space left vacant for your firm's mission statement. A mission statement is not a goal, but rather an idealistic representation of what you see as the fundamental purpose of your firm.

It has been said that a mission statement is a constitution of sorts, and the more it sounds like flag waving, apple pie, and the Fourth of July, the better. It is meant to act as the guiding light.

Because the purpose of a mission statement is to give each person in your firm an understanding of the soul of your practice, it is imperative that it be adopted by the firm as a whole. Each lawyer, secretary, paralegal, messenger, file clerk, receptionist—*everyone* should have the opportunity to place his or her imprint on the mission statement, and it should be adopted by unanimous consent. A mission statement should never be issued by fiat or drafted by one partner. Each person in the firm should know that the mission statement was created, in part, by him or her, and that they are truly members incorporate in its mystical body, as well as its day-to-day operation.

A mission statement for a small law firm or sole practitioner might be something like:

> We, at the law firm of Smith & Jones, adopt this as our Mission Statement: To provide our clients with the highest quality in legal services; To provide our community with support without regard to compensation; To recognize our commitment to justice and fairness in our dealings with all; To recognize that each of us has worth that transcends our job descriptions and thus we must treat each other as we would have others treat us; To be ever mindful of the fact that our clients' welfare is paramount; To recognize that our system of justice is dependent upon each of us to abide by the Canons of Ethics and the rules of the various courts; and, To continually strive to meet the highest standards of conduct and service in both our professional and personal lives.

The problem with many mission statements is that once they are written, they are forgotten. A mission statement, if it is to be a guiding light, must be omnipresent. It should be framed where it can remind each person in your firm of what it is that binds you together in the practice of law. And, if you publish a client newsletter, it's a good idea to repeat it there, too, to let clients know how you view the practice of law.

Marketing Plan of Smith & Jones

Mission Statement:

Overall Goal (include date by which it is to be achieved):

Additional Skills Required to Meet This Goal, if Any:

    Will skills be developed or hired?

        How and by what date will they be developed or hired?

            Set goals for acquiring the additional skills.

                Can skills be developed or hired?

                    If not, abandon goal.

                      If so, continue.

Additional Equipment Required to Meet This Goal, if Any:

    How and by what date will the additional equipment required be obtained?

        Set goals for acquiring the additional equipment.

            Can required equipment be obtained?

                If not, abandon goal.

                  If so, continue.

What Competition Do We Have in Meeting This Goal?

    Analyze the competition.

        Can we perform the service better than the competition?

If not, abandon goal.

If so, continue.

Will the Marketplace Support Our Attaining This Goal?

What is the market for the new (or expanded) service?

What share of that market can we realistically expect to enjoy?

How will this market change in the future?

Is the share large enough to make our goal attainable?

If not, abandon goal.

If so, continue.

What Advertising Efforts Are Necessary to Accomplish This Goal?

Radio? Television? Newspaper? Direct Mail? Other print? (Consult as necessary).

What is the cost of developing the required advertising?

Can we afford this cost?

If not, examine other forms of gaining exposure, below.

If so, set goal to engage advertising firm to prepare campaign, if necessary. Otherwise, plan campaign.

What Public Relations Efforts Are Necessary to Accomplish This Goal?

Radio? Television? Newspaper? Direct Mail? Other print? (Consult as necessary).

What is the cost of developing the required public relations?

Can we afford this cost?

If not, examine other forms of gaining exposure, below.

If so, set goals to engage public relations firm to prepare campaign, if necessary. Otherwise, plan campaign.

What Community Relations Efforts Are Required to Accomplish This Goal?

Analyze community relations efforts. Brainstorm and benchmark as necessary to develop ideas. Consult as necessary.

Can we afford this cost?

If not, abandon goal if all forms of necessary exposure are not affordable. Otherwise, implement other forms (advertising, public relations, e.g., if their effectiveness is not hampered).

If so, set goals to put community relations plan into effect. Consult as necessary.

What Internal Training of Staff Is Required to Accomplish This Goal?

List required training and individuals who must receive the training.

How can this training be achieved most cost-effectively within the time frame required?

What is the cost of this training?

Can we afford this cost?

If not, abandon goal.

If so, set goals to obtain required training.

What Changes and Improvements in Client Relations Will Be Required to Accomplish This Goal?

Analyze client-relations needs from surveys. Conduct surveys as required. Benchmark as required to determine requirements.

How will these changes be implemented?

Can we afford to make these changes?

If not, abandon goal.

If so, set goals for implementing changes and improvements.

How Can We Track the Success of All of These Efforts?

Build in procedures to determine the effectiveness of all steps taken to accomplish the goals.

Measure the effectiveness of each strategy.

Alter strategies to maintain effectiveness.

Abandon strategies that are ineffective.

Obtain client feedback on efforts periodically, both formally and informally.

Change efforts to meet client expectations of quality.

Implement Plan

Delegate authority as required to ensure that plan is implemented as smoothly as possible.

Conduct periodic reviews of plan's implementation, as required.

Make changes to plan as required.

Chapter Three

Focus on Quality and Productivity

WHAT IS TOTAL QUALITY MANAGEMENT?

There are those who regard "Total Quality Management" as just another buzzword, just another fad. But it's not a fad. It's a return to basics where each person is a craftsman, intent on creating the best possible product and improving that product with each subsequent attempt.

For the lawyer, TQM is a focus on what the client needs rather than what the lawyer would like to deliver. It is a focus away from self and on the client, from being master to being servant.

Just as consumers in the last decade grew more willing to question the decisions and treatment programs of their physicians, they are less apt to blindly follow the dictates of their counselors. Empowered by TQM programs in the workplace where, as employees, they are regarded as owners and are respected for individual abilities rather than titles or offices, consumers look for similar empowerment when purchasing goods and services in the marketplace. They recognize and refuse to accept waste, greed, and inefficiency in the services they are offered.

Today the American public judges professionals by their work ethic, by their ability to reach shared goals as a team member, and by their productivity; not by the diplomas that decorate spacious office walls or lavish displays of executive perks.

They demand excellence of themselves and of those who provide them with needed goods and services.

They are familiar with TQM, the American answer to the Japanese quest for excellence that literally shook US business, as a conscious and unrelenting attempt to be as cost-effective and customer-oriented as possible, while still delivering the highest quality in goods or services.

In short, TQM gives the client the best service at the lowest price. It's that basic. The reason no one thought of it before is that the client didn't demand it. Now the client does.

And the lawyer must accede to those demands.

INVOLVE YOUR CLIENTS IN THE DECISION-MAKING PROCESS

There was a time, not so long ago, that a lawyer could simply tell his client what he or she should do and the client would do it. If the client questioned the lawyer's judgment, the result might have been an arrogant display of pique as though to say, "How dare you question me!" As Carl Liggio, chief counsel for the accounting firm of Ernst & Young, once said, "Ten years ago, if you asked for a bill breakdown, the major firms would tell you to stuff it. Now you get whatever you want."

Today, the lawyer who wants to make clients for life will involve them in the decision-making process for a variety of reasons. First, it's in recognition of the fact that the decision is really the client's decision after all, not the lawyer's. It is the client, or his business, that will thrive or suffer to some degree by adopting any particular course of action the lawyer recommends, whether it's in the drafting of a simple contract or the trial of a medical malpractice claim.

Second, clients who are involved in the process will be more willing to help the lawyer understand all of the underpinnings of their needs, knowledge that will help the lawyer make suggestions tailored to their particular and unique circumstances.

When very inexperienced, I drafted what I thought to be a textbook-perfect will for a client I barely knew. It took advantage of every conceivable nuance of the federal tax laws, including those available for married couples.

When the will was completed, I sat across the table from the client and discussed all of its points with him in detail. He looked at me with resignation, as though something horrible had happened. I asked him if something was wrong, and, to my surprise, he told me that he didn't like his wife and wanted to leave as little as possible to her. When I asked him why he hadn't mentioned anything about it before then, he simply shrugged and said, "You never asked." I had been so interested in creating the instrument I wanted to create that I lost sight of what it was my client wanted.

Third, by involving your client in the decision-making process, you get to know each other better. That simple fact makes it harder for him to go elsewhere when he needs legal services in the future. He doesn't have to take the time and expense to educate the next lawyer about his business or personal life. You already know him. You're more productive as a result.

And fourth, and most important, as you and the client share more information, you will grow to trust each other. Mutual respect and trust, of course, form the basis of the lawyer-client relationship.

When there is more than one possible solution to a client's problem (and isn't there almost always?), give her the options in writing, detailing the benefits and detriments of each as well as the estimated costs in time and money. If you wish, recommend the course of action that you feel is best, but let her choose the one she feels is better suited to her needs.

GET TO KNOW YOUR CLIENT'S BUSINESS

If your practice involves representing clients who are in business, you should make a concerted attempt to learn as much as you can about their businesses. Clients today look to their attorneys for business as well as strictly legal advice. They want your guidance to increase profits and to learn what day-to-day impact new laws and regulations will have on their bottom line.

Ask to tour his or her plant on your own time, and meet the workers. You'll gain a valuable appreciation of what your client's world is all about.

Become familiar with your client's industry and competition. Read the trade magazines covering the marketplace where he or she must compete and train yourself to view recent court decisions through your client's eyes. Clip articles of interest to him or her and send them on.

Before you meet with a new client, you should learn as much as possible about his or her business, too. Requesting a copy of the company's annual report will indicate to the potential client your sincere interest. Use your local library's automated retrieval system to locate magazine and newspaper articles about prospective clients and their industries, as well as stories about their competitors.

The more knowledge you have about your client's world, the better able you will be to serve him or her.

BE A "PARTNER"

You should strive to become a partner with your business client and view your relationship with him or her as a symbiotic one. After all, as the client's business grows, so will his or her need for your services.

To stress the fact that you want to be his partner, make it a point to say "we" when you discuss matters. Too much use of the first person singular limits the client's opportunity to become involved in the conversation. It's demeaning to pay someone $100 an hour and then be forced to listen as he pontificates on his virtues, skills, knowledge, and abilities. Think "we." Let clients know that you are willing to share in their problems and solutions. The more you think "we," the more you and your client will become a team.

Marketing your services means making yourself more valuable to your client than any other attorney can.

SAVE YOUR CLIENT MONEY AND TIME

Whether your client is in business or has come to you with a personal or criminal matter, strive to seek the most cost-effective solution, assuming you're looking for repeat business.

The lawyer who tells a client that his problems can be taken care of without expensive legal fees and protracted litigation will have a client for life. In fact, there are times when a client will accept a less attractive, yet cost-effective solution.

When it comes to billing for your services, put yourself in your clients' shoes. Would you pay a paralegal $50 an hour to staple pleadings or provide other services that are clerical in nature and should be included in your nonbillable overhead? Would you pay an associate $100 an hour to do paralegal work? If I spent two minutes on the phone with my lawyer and was charged for 15 minutes because that is the minimum billing period, I would change lawyers. Wouldn't you? I would be furious if I found that my lawyer was billing two clients for the same hour, one for the time spent traveling and one for the work that was done on the plane.

And can you think of a reason why a client should pay a surcharge for messenger or fax services, or a partner's time for reviewing the billing? Neither can I, and neither would your client. In an article in *Colorado Business Magazine,* for example, it was reported that law firms in New

York were billing their own messengers out at $22 an hour, while competing messenger services in Manhattan charged a scant $5.95 an hour for the same service.

If you must travel on behalf of your client, stay in moderately priced hotels, drive, or take the train if it's cheaper, and, if you must go by air, book early to take advantage of the lowest fares, and go coach. The back of the airplane gets there almost as soon as the nose.

Bear in mind that the client who believes that you have taken unfair advantage of him will talk about you, and people will believe him. He may pay the first bill, but it will be the last.

Loren Wittner, the marketing partner at the Chicago-based firm of Winston & Strawn, and an acknowledged expert in the field of law firm marketing, believes that "in order to sustain and enhance client relationships [in the future, firms will] have to provide innovative, win-win fee arrangements and then be able to manage our resources to ensure that they are profitable."

Providing fee arrangements that are attractive to clients, indeed, even providing prospective clients with detailed, firm estimates of the prospective costs of services, is something small firms should also strive to do.

AVOID LITIGATION IF POSSIBLE

Litigation is costly, and there is a tremendous surge of interest among large companies to seek alternative means of dispute resolution. Some 600 major corporations have entered into an agreement not to sue each other unless less costly means to resolve their differences have failed. Richard H. Weise, general counsel of Motorola Corporation, demands that the 100 or so lawyers who work for him try such methods as arbitration, mediation, even the hiring of retired judges to settle disputes, with each side agreeing in advance to abide by the decision rendered. Weise makes going to litigation a last resort option.

According to an article in *Business Week,* Weise's efforts have paid off. Motorola's litigation costs have been reduced by as much as 75 percent.

The fear of litigation and the costs associated with lawsuits are having a deleterious effect on corporate America's ability to compete with foreign companies, according to that article. Dow Chemical, for example, reportedly spends more than $100 million each year in legal services and liability insurance, according to its assistant general counsel, Ronald L.

Davis, who is quoted in the article as saying that "The American economy can no longer afford this process. The [legal] system's inefficiencies are eating away at our industrial base."

A study conducted by the Rand corporation estimates the total cost of the American tort system—court expenses, legal fees, lost work time, and so on—at more than *$51 billion* each year.

The effects of such unproductive spending trickle down to small businesses and individuals as well, in terms of jobs that are not created, orders that are not placed, plants that close, and improvements in safety and plant modernization that are not made.

By seeking alternative dispute resolution means, you stand to save your client, and the rest of America, time, money, and a more secure future in the global marketplace.

In Japan, for example, suits between companies are extremely rare. According to an article in *Business Week,* "Lower [legal] bills free up cash for research and other areas, and enable more competitive pricing than US companies can afford."

Lawyers who are adept at saving their clients needless expenditures will find that they are also adept at obtaining and retaining clients.

TELL YOUR CLIENTS THE "WHY" OF THINGS

For your client to make informed decisions, he or she must know why you recommend certain courses of action over others. It also allows the client to consider business and/or personal considerations that you may well be unaware of.

To make sure that your client understands what you tell him, follow up your telephone or face-to-face conversations with a brief letter describing what was said. If there's a problem, you'll hear about it when it can still be avoided, saving embarrassment later.

USE YOUR TIME BETTER

You can't create time, but you can make better use of it. First, don't think in terms of hours, but in terms of minutes. Saving a minute here and a minute there will soon add up to savings of hours that you can put to productive use.

Where do you find minutes to save? Try these ideas:

1. Don't engage in a conversation that is not job related. If someone wants to talk about last night's basketball game, appear busy. They'll get the message and respect your time more.

2. When there is an interruption, control it before it controls you. If a personal telephone call is the culprit, explain to the caller that you can't talk, say goodbye, and hang up. You have the right to control the length of the call.

3. If you have time on your hands, tackle a job that needs to get done, rather than spending it on routine tasks that can wait.

4. If you're a morning person, work on the most challenging job in the morning, when you're at your best. If you're an afternoon person, work on that job then. You'll find it takes less time to get things done when you're sharpest.

5. Don't start a half-hour job when you only have 10 minutes. You'll only have to start it over again. Schedule your time wisely, then start on time and finish on time.

6. Set your own deadlines, and make them tougher than anyone else would. Then meet them, consistently. With a little bit of self-discipline, you'll surprise everyone with what you can do. You'll even surprise yourself.

7. Got a tough or distasteful job to do? Don't put it off. Do it now, so it won't be hanging over your head as a reminder of the way you *used* to work. If you can't get to it right away, make an appointment with yourself to get it done on a certain date and do it.

8. Don't think of the clock. Concentrate on production, not minutes. Minutes pass faster when you're busy, and you'll feel better when you're more productive.

9. Keep notes. Write down ideas to discuss with your partner, associate, secretary, or paralegal. When you have five items, go and see them. Don't waste your time or theirs with meetings or unnecessary interruptions unless there is something that can't wait.

10. Make your time at work just that—time for work. Besides being more productive, you'll set the example for the people who work with you.

Remember, time is a resource, just like wood for the cabinetmaker or steel for the auto maker. Manage it well, with as little waste as possible. The one who wastes the least is the best craftsman.

Another way to successfully manage time is to keep a listing of everything you do for two weeks, even the inconsequential. Have others in your office do the same.

At the end of the period, go through the list and see what items can be eliminated altogether, things that take time but yield nothing. Resolve never to do them again, and take steps to keep that promise.

Then examine what you do that could be done just as well by someone else, things like clerical chores. Delegate the responsibility for such chores to your associate, paralegal, or other support staff so you can get on with what you should be doing: practicing law and planning for the future success of your firm.

LEARN HOW TO DELEGATE EFFECTIVELY

It's not easy to give up authority to others, but it's necessary to your success as a leader.

"Sometimes it's awful," says Debi Fields, CEO of cookie giant Mrs. Fields, Inc., in *Working Woman* magazine. "I've agreed to things up front knowing full well I didn't like them. I have to constantly remind myself to be open-minded, not to say no. You have to let people make decisions in spite of what your gut tells you, as long as they're not betting the farm."

Fields had no choice but to relinquish much of the hands-on, day-to-day management of her company as it grew from a $200,000 a year bakery to an international firm with sales over $100 million in just 10 years. Changing the light bulbs in 600 stores is an impossible task for one person.

But before Fields delegated the authority to make decisions to others, she made sure they knew their jobs and the expectations she had for them. About one such hire she says, "I had to be sure he cared about people. I had to make sure he knew how to make good cookies."

'Fields' initial reluctance to delegate authority is common among those responsible for the supervision of others and for productivity. "If you want it done right, do it yourself" is an axiom that we have all heard.

Today's fast-paced marketplace, however, complex as it is, no longer allows the boss the time and flexibility to make all the decisions. He or she must delegate decision-making responsibility to others, freeing time to spend on developing the big picture. If you want it done right today, you can't do it all by yourself.

How can you learn to delegate? In his book, *Manage More By Doing Less* (McGraw-Hill), author Raymond O. Loen says "the best single way to make sure you delegate well is to *stress results more than methods.*" Let people develop their own ways to design, sell, and produce, providing, however, as Fields learned, that you "distinguish and make clear the results you want."

Loen lists five steps to follow to delegate effectively:

1. Implement your organization plan. Make sure that everyone knows what day-to-day tasks will be delegated to whom.

2. Avoid making routine decisions. Let your associates, paraprofessionals, and clerical staff make the decisions, so long as they have an understanding of what you want to have done.

3. Get your staff's recommendations. They know their jobs if you have trained them well.

4. Have your key people with you in meetings so they know what the future will demand of them.

5. Avoid overdelegating. Train people in their new responsibilities and never delegate important functions to them until they are ready to handle their new responsibilities.

But remember that delegating does not mean giving all authority away. As Fields says, "I come with a warning. I tell people up front, 'I need to be involved. If you think I'm meddling in your business, I am.'" At least until she's sure they know what she wants.

HOW WELL DO YOU DELEGATE?

While delegating authority isn't a science—it depends upon the authority delegated and the person to whom it is delegated—there are some factors you can examine to see if you're delegating well. Your score in the quiz on the next page will tell you not only how you're doing, but where you may need to improve. Simply answer each question Yes or No.

MAKE QUALITY EVERYONE'S FOCUS

Perhaps the most important job you have in making quality a way of life in the workplace is making sure that it is everybody's job, and not just yours alone. And one way to make it everyone's focus is to give them the power to be more than what you expect them to be.

People live up to the expectations others have of them. If you think that Sally will have five errors per page of typing, Sally will live up to that

	Yes	*No*

1. Are you sure that the person to whom you have delegated authority has a clear understanding of the problem?

2. Have you set high standards in the past that make it clear what performance you will demand now?

3. Have you demonstrated in the past that you trust the delegate's judgment?

4. Do you have a track record of jumping in at the last minute to pull others' irons out of the fire?

5. Do you avoid attending meetings just to "make sure he or she is doing it right?"

6. Do you require excessive progress reports?

7. When asked for guidance, do you give orders instead?

8. Do you make it clear that the ball is in the delegate's court, and you will not interfere unnecessarily?

9. Have you given the delegate formal authority (such as a dollar sign-off level) so he or she isn't required to check with you about trivial matters?

10. Do you ignore gossip that says the delegate is "in over his or her head?"

Score Yourself: The preferred answers to this quiz are: 1. Yes; 2. Yes; 3. Yes; 4. No; 5. Yes; 6. No; 7. No; 8. Yes; 9. Yes; and 10. Yes. If your answers do not agree, you may not be letting go enough to allow the delegate the freedom to use his or her own abilities fully.

expectation. If you let her know that your expectation is an error-free document, and give her feedback, positive and negative as required, she will eventually deliver error-free work.

If you demand quality from your coworkers, you will get it. People want to do their work well. They want to receive credit for a job well done. They want to take pride in what they do. And they want the respect of their peers, superiors, and subordinates for the way in which they do their work.

One of the greatest mistakes supervisors at all levels make is to demand less than the best an individual can produce. It detracts from the individual's drive to succeed, the supervisor's ability to reach his or her goals, and the firm's ability to remain competitive.

In demanding the highest quality from people in your office, you are giving them the opportunity to develop and grow in their positions. That is an essential element in increasing employee job satisfaction and productivity.

TEAM MEETINGS

To empower your coworkers to greater productivity and to enhance the quality of the services your office provides its clients, you should involve every person in the firm in monthly team meetings. Discuss where quality can be improved, problems that affect productivity, and the quality of life in the workplace, as well as other opportunities for change that can make your workplace a better place to work.

The rules for a team meeting are relatively simple. First, there should be no disparaging remarks made by anyone. Everyone must feel free to make comments and suggestions. Second, promise that every idea presented will be considered. The first time an individual's idea is rejected as stupid will be the last time an idea is heard from that person. Third, there is no rank in the meeting. No one's ideas have greater worth than anyone else's. Fourth, have an agenda prepared for the meeting. Each person on staff has the obligation to contribute agenda items before the meeting. A copy of the agenda should be given to everyone well in advance of the meeting so that they have the opportunity to reflect upon the subject matters to be discussed. Fifth, stick to the agenda. Finally, there must be no retaliation for anything that is said in the meeting. If a mistake is brought up, it should be viewed as an opportunity for all to learn from, and never as a reason to punish an individual. If you punish honest mistakes, people will still make them; they just won't let you know about them.

Team meetings can be a wonderful opportunity for everyone to share their most creative ideas, to solve problems, and develop their abilities to see their jobs in the context of the firm as a whole. Active participants who are accepted as members of a team will be more loyal and devoted to the accomplishment of team goals than those who are regarded as having merely a job.

Some subjects that should be brought up at every team meeting include the following:

1. In what way can client services be improved? (Encourage the use of examples in which clients were handled in the past month and look for suggestions as to how situations could be better handled.)

2. In what way can costs be contained? (Encourage small cost-saving suggestions, like the use of ceramic mugs rather than styrofoam cups, but don't ignore the larger opportunities for savings, such as investigating the purchase of new computers and/or software that makes work faster and more accurate.)

3. How can productivity be enhanced? (Can some jobs that are repetitive be automated? Can one person's downtime be used to help in other areas that seem overloaded? Can time not utilized fully be put to better use? Can some tasks be eliminated altogether?)

4. What progress is being made in implementing our marketing plan? (Are all intermediate goal deadlines being met? Are changes to any goal required? Are tracking procedures and devices being monitored? What feedback are we receiving? What can we do to make the plan more effective?)

5. Make sure you can single out at least one thing each coworker in the firm has done since the last meeting to praise. Never use a team meeting as a forum to correct or discipline behavior. And share news that you have with your team, both the good and the bad. Leaders who share information will be trusted more by their coworkers, who will in turn more readily share their news with you.

TREAT EVERYONE LIKE A CUSTOMER

You, and everyone in your firm, are dependent on each other for success. If you view each person in your firm as the owner of his or her own small business, and encourage others to do so also, productivity and quality will be enhanced.

Fred will no longer be an intern whose job is to research land use law. Now he is the owner of a legal research firm and you are one of his customers. Pleasing you, giving you the quality you demand, is his business, and one that he owns.

Similarly, Sally, the receptionist, is now an answering service. You will use her services so long as she does her job in a way that reflects well upon your firm. Because she wants to keep you as a customer, she will look for ways to improve the quality of her service.

And Gladys, the file clerk, is now the sole proprietor of an information retrieval system company.

As each person in your firm sees their job as one in which they have an ownership interest, and feels that they have the power to control their destinies to some extent, they will work harder to keep you happy as a customer.

QUALITY IS NEVER ACHIEVED; PRODUCTIVITY CAN ALWAYS BE IMPROVED

The one immutable truth about quality is that it can never be totally achieved. There will always be changes in client needs, business, the law, the marketplace, technology, the community, the people you work with, competition—changes that will make perfection elusive. The goal is to constantly improve. And that is attainable.

Likewise, productivity can always be improved, but will never reach the point where improvements are no longer possible. The goal here is to constantly seek ways in which to do more with less. And that, too, is attainable.

Our focus, then, must always be on quality and productivity because the quest to achieve them is never-ending.

Chapter Four

Client Relations

"The client is always right."

Anonymous

"What does a [client] want?"

Sigmund Freud *(Paraphrased)*

Law firm marketing professionals in large firms refer to their efforts in a variety of ways: client development, new business development, client relations, client services, practice development, and, sometimes, marketing. But the one thing each of the programs has in common, despite the moniker, is a focus on improving the manner in which they deal with clients—prospective, current, and past.

TOTAL QUALITY MANAGEMENT IN CLIENT RELATIONS

A survey conducted in 1993 by *Of Counsel* magazine indicated that nearly one-third of all responding firms (32.4 percent of 146 law firms) was engaged in a total quality management ("TQM") program. Of the remaining two-thirds, nearly half had some form of formal marketing training program in effect.

The survey accurately reported that "There is a natural relationship between TQM and marketing; a law firm, for example, must communicate better with clients in order to determine how to meet or, ideally, exceed client expectations."

Of course, there is more to TQM than communications. The hallmarks of the program are to continually strive to improve the quality of doing what you do, to do every task as error-free as possible, to become as streamlined and productive as possible, to pass on your savings to your clients in terms of better, more cost-effective service, and to make client satisfaction your primary goal.

Total Quality Management utilizes a number of different, teamwork-oriented, problem-solving techniques that bear mention here, if only for the reason that they can help your office work together more effectively, and efficiently, toward meeting client needs.

Among those techniques are *benchmarking, brainstorming,* and *huddling.*

Benchmarking

Through benchmarking, a TQM initiative that, according to the *Of Counsel* survey, is derided by some firms as more appropriate in a manufacturing context, a firm may learn how to collect billings more efficiently, install a more effective local area network for their word processing and other computer-based operations, or create a training program that draws upon the expertise of companies involved heavily in sales to professionals, such as life insurance and stock brokerage companies.

Benchmarking does not have to be concerned solely with the delivery of legal services. And the entity that is benchmarked does not have to be another law firm. L.L. Bean, Maine's famous direct-mail purveyor of high-quality outdoor goods, is a favorite benchmark for those in the business of filling mail and telephone orders, including major automobile parts suppliers, who marveled at the simplicity of Bean's success: The goods ordered most frequently were stored nearest the order desk. Hence, it took less time at the end of the day to find and ship those items. What can a law firm learn from the L.L. Bean example?

By cutting down on the number of steps employees must take to accomplish routine tasks, productivity will improve. Moving the most commonly accessed file nearer to the people who use it most frequently will result in less time wasted. Is this client relations? If it contributes to a faster client-response time or lower billings for work performed more efficiently, it is.

And, of course, benchmarking can be used to discover new ways to solve legal problems as well. By studying the manner in which a respected trial lawyer makes opening statements, interrogates witnesses, and maintains eye contact with a jury, the new lawyer may learn isolated examples of how the craft is plied. But by benchmarking the trial attorney, the neophyte will be able to understand the outward signs and actions in the context of the trial strategy as a whole, a feat that, without benchmarking, could take years to comprehend.

Using Brainstorming to Solve Client Problems

TQM advocates believe that teams should be created to tackle problems, and team members who brainstorm effectively can often find creative solutions to client problems.

According to *Industry Week* magazine, Steelcase, a company under the leadership of Frank Merlotti, organized nearly 90 percent of its 5,400 employees into 560 work teams and encouraged them to brainstorm. Any problem, according to Merlotti, whether it is "a recurring annoyance or interferes with productivity, or wastes time" gets put on the list of problems to be brainstormed by teams that elect their own leaders. During the first year of the program, savings amounted to $1.2 million.

Brainstorming gives the guys in the trenches the impetus to get involved in identifying problems as well as in assisting in their solution, says Merlotti, who recalls one employee in a distribution area who, during his first experience as a member of a team, came up with an idea that saved the company $150,000.

How does a team brainstorm effectively? In *Teamwork: Involving People in Quality and Productivity Improvement* by Charles A. Aubrey II and Patricia K. Felkins, the authors set the basic guidelines for "round-robin" brainstorming to ensure equal participation:

- Each member, in rotation, is asked for ideas to solve the problem. This continues until all members run out of ideas.
- Each member offers only one idea per turn.
- Members can pass on their turn if they don't have an idea.
- There should not be any evaluation of suggested ideas, positive or negative, during brainstorming. This applies to team leaders, too.
- And no idea should ever be treated as silly or wrong. Great discoveries have been known to come from strange ideas.

Later, when the session is over, the team is free to evaluate the ideas generated during the brainstorming session and, by vote or consensus, choose those they believe most viable.

Such sessions help members unleash their creativity without fear of criticism. They also permit those team members with hands-on experience in the problem areas—secretarial, paraprofessional and clerical staff, for example—to suggest solutions senior management might never consider.

Team leaders should make sure that their team members understand the guidelines before participating in a brainstorming exercise so that members feel free to suggest any solution, even if it is, in fact, silly.

As Aubrey and Felkins say, "All ideas, no matter how exaggerated, should be encouraged. Exaggeration may be humorous, but it adds a creative stimulus to the process. Likewise, a touch of fantasy can help shed the bonds that prevent members from thinking creatively."

Using this approach is client relations, too, if its effect is to find creative solutions to a client's problem or if it makes the firm more efficient and, therefore, more competitively priced.

Huddling for Success

Huddling: football teams do it before every play to make sure everyone knows what the team will do next. It's also a powerful tool for work groups to use to solve client problems in a creative and time-saving way that builds team spirit.

"People in huddles usually accomplish the most significant work in organizations," says V. Dallas Merrell in *Huddling: The Informal Way To Management Success* (AMACOM). He defines huddling as "a temporary, intimate, work-oriented encounter between two or more people."

"Huddlers," Merrell says, "draw together informally and confer, 'nestling' to get results where organizations fail. A huddle is the source of considerable information, the locus of significant decisions, the setting for power transactions, the place where many responsibilities get defined, and the impetus for motivating people to get things done. Huddlers compensate for countless organizational ineptitudes."

Why does huddling accomplish so much? The informal nature of these meetings allows for more intimate contact, the ability to exercise influence and to share information that would be difficult to share in more structured meetings. In short, huddling removes the walls that sometime impede direct communications and allows individuals to be more candid with each other.

"Organizations don't work well normally," says Merrell. "Everyone knows that. Throughout our lives virtually all of us confront perplexing, formalistic, phlegmatic organizations. Yet some organizational workers manage to accomplish more than others, to get results in spite of the formal organization. Sometimes we forget that organizations don't get results, people do!"

Merrell likens huddling to natural streams and tributaries, unlike engineered channels of communication. "Left alone," he says, "communication will flow in natural patterns through areas of least resistance. Like a stream of water winding through a mountain valley, communication moves from person to person and huddle to huddle wherever the message can get through."

Huddling, Merrell postulates, is just another way of getting people together to obtain the results you want. And, of course, it increases productivity.

USING THE CLIENT RELATIONSHIP FOR FEEDBACK

A report issued by the consulting firm Hildebrandt, Inc. states that "Law firms that fail to see the value of asking clients to evaluate their performance are shortsighted.

"Client assessment surveys have been initiated by a growing number of firms, frequently enabling them to revitalize client relationships that otherwise would have languished or died," the study reported.

The utility of client assessment surveys is not, however, limited to what they can do to repair or breathe life into a relationship that is in trouble. These surveys can be beneficial in uncovering trends in areas where improvements can be made. For one client to respond that your offices are located in an area of town that is hard to access may be the result of difference of opinion about what "accessible" means. If a great many of your clients complain, however, that they find coming to your office difficult because of lack of parking, for example, it may be time to consider relocating.

And the surveys can also point up problems in personnel. Some firms ask their clients to help them rate associates' performance, allowing them to see the associate through the eyes of a client.

Client assessment surveys, and the use of focus groups (small groups of clients who meet with firm personnel to discuss ways in which service can be improved), can be valuable tools for repairing, strengthening, and creating ties with clients. Use of these tools also reinforces the impression in the client's mind that the firm is truly interested in achieving greater quality in the service it provides.

BROCHURES AND NEWSLETTERS

According to the *Of Counsel* survey, nearly 95 percent of the responding firms used a brochure for marketing purposes, and almost 80 percent of those brochures were revised within the preceding 12 months. Ninety percent of the firms provided their clients with a newsletter.

As will be discussed more fully in Chapter 7, small firms and sole practitioners may wish to publish their own newsletters, or they may buy preprinted newsletters from entities such as the American Bar Association. Newsletters should offer clients something of value, and should not be seen primarily as a sales piece.

Brochures, however, are a different matter. They should be created, where allowed, as a direct-mail marketing piece to highlight your firm's unique qualifications, skills, and abilities to handle specific tasks. It is not unreasonable to expect that even a small firm may have more than one brochure to offer prospective clients, particularly if the lawyers who work there have different interests and experience, or if they are marketing their services to more than one type of client.

Brochures may be as simple as a tri-fold self-mailer or as complex as a full-color piece with professional photography. What is important, however, is that the brochure fills a need that the client has rather than strokes the egos of the senior partners who commission its creation. Glitzy, self-touting mailings often end up in the wastebasket, unread, by in-house counsel who are used to having such publications cross their desks.

Client testimonials about the value of the services they have received from your firm can be effective, particularly if the client and the prospective client are in the same line of work (manufacturing or retail sales, for example), or, in the event that yours is a plaintiff's practice, a former client's statement that he or she was satisfied with the outcome of their case. The danger there, of course, is that you do not want to hint that you can guarantee an outcome similar to that client's.

CLIENT SEMINARS

The *Of Counsel* survey reports that more than 95 percent of the responding firms held seminars for clients and prospective clients. There is no reason why small firms and sole practitioners cannot also offer seminars on topics of interest to their clients and prospective clients.

Again, however, keep in mind that you must offer something of value to the client. Company and departmental heads receive many invitations to such gatherings and their schedules often will not permit them to attend.

Instead of relying on the key players to attend, you might wish to hold a seminar and invite the "wrong" people.

Imagine offering companies in your area workshops *for their employees* on such subjects as "Sexual Harassment in the Workplace—It Can Cost You Your Job" or "The Americans with Disabilities Act—It's Every Manager's Job."

A plaintiff's lawyer might offer seminars to the general public on such topics as "Medical Malpractice: What Is It?" or "Are You At Risk For Repetitive Motion? Your Rights Under Workers' Compensation," or similar topics consistent with his or her experience and interests.

The seminars should be advertised far enough in advance of the event to prepare adequately for the number of participants that accept. RSVPs are advised to prevent embarrassingly low head counts (you can cancel a seminar for a party of one), to make sure that you have sufficient numbers of handouts (including firm brochures and newsletter copies relevant to the subject matter), to prepare the meeting area to most comfortably and effectively seat the participants (lecture style, round-table, a conference with active participants?), to plan for refreshments, and to measure the effectiveness of the advertising, especially if more than one form of advertising has been used.

Use visual and hands-on, interactive aids to keep the pace of the seminar at a comfortable but energetic level. Rehearse your presentation so that you do not have to rely on notes, flip charts, or overhead slides to keep you on track. How you deliver your presentation is just as important as its content.

Allow time for questions at the end, but have an encore planned in the event questions are sparse. Also leave time for the participants to fill out a questionnaire that rates your performance, the topic covered, usefulness of the seminar, whether they would attend similar conferences in the future, and similar evaluation questions. Their responses can be used in later promotional brochures and in helping you adapt future seminars to meet their expectations, as well as for your personal growth.

You can also use the tips under the heading "Make Client Meetings Work For You" later in this chapter to help you plan a seminar that will be remembered.

CLIENT APPRECIATION DAYS

Client appreciation days, whether they are disguised as cocktail parties near the holidays, picnics, golf outings, dinner cruises, barbecues, or a "bring your spouse and kids to the local amusement park day," can be a valuable way to create a relaxed and enjoyable atmosphere with your clients, and an event they will remember and look forward to sharing again each year.

Obviously, the types of activity will vary tremendously, depending upon the clients to be entertained and the money you are willing to spend. But the less businesslike the event, the better.

At the end of the event, you might consider giving each client and prospective client some small memento of the occasion, preferably something that they might use frequently, such as a coffee mug with your firm's name and telephone number and the words "In Appreciation of Your Trust," for example, printed on it.

One caveat about client appreciation days, parties, and similar affairs. Pull from the list of clients those with whom you have difficulty, whether it's a fee dispute or something more serious. The last thing you need at your party is someone who will use the event to bad-mouth your firm to other clients.

USE REFRESHMENTS TO AID CLIENT RELATIONS

Janet Reich, the owner of a management firm in Colorado, feels that teams, such as the teams you are attempting to build with your clients, benefit from bonding in much the same way as families do. Serving refreshments at meetings helps, she says, because even the simple act of sharing food as a family unit can create psychological attachments.

She also observes that effective team builders avoid the "I" and "my" words and use liberal doses of "we" and "our" in their stead, stressing the shared nature of their relationship.

Teams that bond predictably tend to work better together, become more productive, last longer, and more quickly attain their goals.

MAKE CLIENT MEETINGS WORK FOR YOU

A good meeting should "leave its participants on a high, feeling resolute and energized," says management consultant Ellen Belzer. In discussions with top executives, she discovered the following tips for making meetings enjoyable as well as productive:

Be positive. Greet everyone warmly as they walk in and act as though you want to be there, too. Be attentive to your body language. Mary Maples Dunn, president of Smith College, told Belzer that when she calls a meeting, she tries to create an environment in which "the tone is so positive, everyone feels good about being there—and we get more accomplished as a result."

Match seating to the meeting. If you want group participation, seat the group in a circle or around a table to maximize eye contact. For an instructional meeting, seat them classroom style.

Keep the meeting on track. Don't let anyone, including yourself, guide the group away from the agenda. Take notes so you know where the meeting started to go astray and so you can lead the group back. Valid points that are not on the agenda can be saved for the next meeting, when everyone has had a chance to consider them.

Use phrases like, "I think we've already decided that," or "We've brought up these three points, now let's talk about . . ." to keep distracting talk to a minimum.

Break the routine. Start with a brief film or slide show for a change, invite a guest speaker, or kick off the meeting with a joke. Find new, interesting, and unexpected ways to keep colleagues interested.

Develop an open atmosphere. "One of the key ingredients of camaraderie and creativity is a nonthreatening atmosphere," says Belzer. "Try to convey to your staff that all ideas are important. Create a brainstorming environment where there are no wrong answers, and, wherever possible, make decisions by consensus rather than vote. (Voting is divisive—one side always loses)."

Share information. Belzer calls those who don't "fact hogs," and stresses that information concerning the team's effort should be shared with everyone who is affected by it, and not just with the key players. Not only does it make staff on all levels feel like a part of the team, it gives them tools to use in their quest to contribute.

Gear up for action. "You should never leave a meeting thinking just, 'Gee, what a great conversation,'" says Dunn. Belzer says that she advises "writing down the names of people who, during the meeting, volunteered to take action on a problem. Then, Dunn says, at the end of the meeting, "hand out the responsibility."

HOW GOOD ARE YOUR MEETINGS?

There are time-honored rules for making meetings productive. Take the self-assessment on the next page to see where you need improvement. You can use it later as a guide for planning and conducting meetings.

Rate your present performance as *Good* or *Need Improvement* after each statement.

The results of this exercise should lead you to understand where you may need to focus attention to brush up your meeting skills.

OFFER TO INVOLVE OTHER PROFESSIONALS WHEN IT IS NECESSARY

As a partner or associate in a small firm, or as a sole practitioner, you most likely will not have the resources to be a single-source provider for all of your client's legal service needs. You cannot be an expert in everything.

You should, therefore, maintain relationships with lawyers, accountants, and other professionals you trust for recommendations when appropriate.

If there are to be meetings with the client and the other professional, it is recommended that you be present. You know your client's needs best and are better able to see the possible ramifications of advice that may be given.

If you do not have an established relationship with a needed professional, meet with several first before suggesting that your client engage their services. Before you broach the subject with your client, you must be satisfied that the one you name is competent and will be a good fit with your client.

Remember, you will be judged not only by the work that you do, but by the work of others whom you recommend. Retain the right to review that work before it is presented to the client.

	Good	*Need Improvement*

1. I develop an objective for each meeting in advance.

2. I prepare myself; I plan the tactics and timetable for the meeting well enough in advance to take care of the unexpected.

3. I decide who should attend based on what agenda items need to be resolved. If other attorneys or paralegals from my office are involved, I make sure the client knows why their presence is required or I tell the client that their time is not being billed.

4. I advise the participants of the time and date of the meeting in time for them to prepare.

5. I have all the necessary papers ready, and circulate them to others who need to see them in advance, and make sure that the handouts for distribution have been checked and rechecked for accuracy and readability.

6. I ensure that necessary arrangements for accommodations and administrative details have been made.

7. I start the meeting on time.

8. I state the purpose of the meeting.

9. I direct the discussion, stage by stage, but allow all to participate freely.

10. I am alert to the feelings and objectives of the participants and steer clear of discussion topics that will unnecessarily offend anyone.

11. I help the group to agree upon specific conclusions at each stage, and strive for unanimity. When there is conflict as to the course to be followed, I advise, but yield gracefully to the desires of my client.

12. I nominate people responsible for action and review, if necessary, and accept tasks for myself to accomplish.

13. I arrange the time and date for follow-up on action or for the next meeting, paying attention to conflicts the other participants may have.

14. I follow up each meeting with a letter to the client detailing the action agreed upon to make sure there are no misunderstandings.

IN A NUTSHELL, TREAT CLIENTS THE WAY YOU WOULD LIKE TO BE TREATED

Adopting the Golden Rule as a basis for interpersonal relationships, especially with your clients and coworkers, is the foundation of a strong client relations program. The following example of a retail enterprise makes this point very clearly.

Doing unto others as you would have them do unto you has helped the Ukrop family Virginia-based grocery store grow into a chain of 22 stores employing more than 4,300 people, according to a story in *Readers' Digest.*

"We trust our customers," Jim Ukrop says. "And they trust us."

If a customer runs out of checks at one of the Ukrop stores, he or she simply signs the register tape and is trusted to pay the next time they are in the store.

Customers with flat tires and dead batteries can expect help from the baggers, and the chain tithes 10 percent of its *pretax* dollars to the community. If that's not enough, Ukrop's Super Markets, Inc. also donates as much as $800,000 each year to charities selected by their customers. And they even decided not to compete with a small frozen yogurt vendor because, as Ukrop says, "We're not out to cause anyone hardship."

Placing such emphasis on customers and community has a profound effect on customer loyalty. "What we're doing, I believe, shows that the Golden Rule really works," Ukrop says.

The attorneys and staffs of small firms and sole practitioners can develop a strong and loyal following among their clients too, simply by treating others with the courtesy, professionalism, and respect they themselves would appreciate.

Your mother was right.

Chapter Five

Public and Community Relations

WHAT ARE PUBLIC AND COMMUNITY RELATIONS?

According to the *Columbia Concise Encyclopedia,* public relations consists in those "activities and policies used to create public interest in a person, idea, product, institution, or business establishment." It "serves particular interests by presenting them to the public in the most favorable light." The "public" that is sought to be influenced can be as specific as the various forms of media and information permit, or as wide as, for example, a television audience.

Community relations programs have the same aim, to create a favorable impression, but in a generally more diffuse target audience, and the messages used to convey the favorable impression are usually of an educational or philanthropic nature.

By presenting interests "in the most favorable light," public relations and community relations programs should never misrepresent. Indeed, public relations professionals are bound by the tenets of their profession to refrain from publicizing false or misleading impressions and, in some cases, are under an affirmative duty to correct misstatements. (See, e.g., *Green* v. *Jonhap,* 358 F.Supp. 413 [D.Ore. 1973]).

PUBLIC RELATIONS

The most commonly used form of public relations is the news release, a story that is written to be read as news. It is sent to the editors of selected newspapers and magazines that will be read by the audience the writer wants to reach.

Effective public relations is dependent not only on the news value of the story (is it something the editors of the publications think their readers will want to read?) and the quality of the writing, but also on the relationship that exists between the writer and the editor to whom the articles are sent.

For those reasons, I would encourage anyone seeking positive public relations coverage to consult with an established public relations professional, skilled in the placement of releases in periodicals and newspapers likely to be read by the public they seek to influence. Obviously, the same style of writing would not be acceptable to both the *ABA Journal* and a technical journal that appeals to petroleum engineers.

Experienced public relations professionals can also help small firms and sole practitioners in devising a comprehensive and integrated public and community relations program.

There are some caveats about dealing with editors when you are trying to get a release published. First, *never* indicate that you will buy an ad in the newspaper or periodical if the story is placed. Not only will the release not get placed, you will never have another placed either. Even though advertising is important to a publication, editorial integrity is more important. It is also unethical in many jurisdictions to offer anything of value in exchange for being mentioned in a news story.

Second, if your release is not printed, don't demand to know why. There is only so much room available in each magazine or newspaper, and editors must make decisions based on what they believe is best for their readership.

And, third, if your release does make it into print, don't complain if the piece had to be edited to fit the space available. If you complain, the editor will be less likely to honor future requests.

COMMUNITY RELATIONS

There are a number of worthwhile endeavors that any community relations budget can support to generate both goodwill and a favorable image in the community served by your practice. *Indeed, the best way to generate positive news in your community about yourself and your firm is to do something positive for your community that is newsworthy.*

The following are merely examples that have been tried and found effective.

Establish a scholarship fund.   For as little as $250 a year, you can establish a scholarship in your firm's name to help a deserving student pay tuition at the college or professional school of his or her choice.

In selecting the criteria for determining who will receive the award, decide in what ways you would like to benefit from the expenditure.

If you want to develop better relations with a local hospital, you may wish to make the award to a nursing or premed student, chosen on the basis of exceptional grades and teacher recommendations.

To appeal to a veterans group, you might sponsor a speech contest in which the subject matter revolves around some aspect of patriotism.

Appealing to educators, a scholarship program might permit the local teachers' association to nominate students planning to become educators.

There is a seemingly unlimited number of opportunities to use the establishment of a scholarship drive as an opportunity to create good relations with some segment of the community in which you work. (See the sample news release at the end of this section announcing the establishment of a scholarship drive.)

Sponsor a Law Day contest.   To encourage awareness of Law Day and the legal profession among schoolchildren of various ages (and hence their teachers and parents), you might wish to start an annual Law Day Program in which a combination of events is used to associate your firm's name with the most honorable aspects of the profession.

You could include a coloring contest (blanks can be purchased in bulk; contact a provider of school supplies) at the lower grade levels, essay contests at the intermediate grade levels, and, perhaps, a moot court competition at the higher grade levels. The latter option, of course, would require a great deal of planning and cooperation with the schools, yet would increase the likelihood of local television coverage.

Likely prizes awarded the winners would be US Savings Bonds, purchased at one-half their face value, or books on the history of the United States legal system.

Sponsor movies on public television.   The cost of sponsoring movies on public television will vary from city to city; the larger the viewing audience, the larger the fee. But it may be the most affordable form of television exposure you can get, and being associated with public television is itself beneficial.

In my city, for $1,600, I can sponsor the Monday through Friday 10:30 "Silver Screen" movie for 13 full weeks. For that sum, I will get a promotional message ("This Programming Is Made Possible by a Grant from Smith & Jones, a Full Service Law Firm Located in Your City") at the beginning and end of each movie. That works out to approximately $12 per message.

For $800, I can sponsor the Saturday night "Movie of the Week" for a full 13 weeks with the same promotional announcements at the beginning and end of the movie. (About $30 per message, but higher quality programming and, it is assumed, a larger viewing audience.)

The station I contacted for this information also told me that I might be able to obtain a special showing of a particular film on a particular date if available. I might, therefore, be able to sponsor *Yankee Doodle Dandy* on the 4th of July, *To Kill a Mockingbird* on Law Day, or *Young Mr. Lincoln* on Presidents' Day.

To take maximum advantage of the opportunity to sponsor PBS programming, small advertisements could be taken out in the local television listing guide stating that, "Tonight, the law firm of Smith & Jones sponsors Harper Lee's film classic, 'To Kill a Mockingbird,' starring Gregory Peck."

Start a people's law school. In conjunction with your local library and county bar association, you can start a people's law school, which offers consumers question and answer panels composed of lawyers in various fields. Generally held in the evening, they are well publicized and scheduled as recurring events, covering different topics at different times during the year.

The cost of starting such a school is minimal; local television and radio stations and newspapers may well be convinced to give free notice of the pending events as a public service. And there will likely be no scarcity of lawyers (in fields other than the one in which you seek to improve gross revenues) willing to participate and share what costs remain.

In some communities, such people's law schools have expanded to become recurring PBS or community television programs.

If your local bar already sponsors a people's law school, become actively involved as a regular participant.

Perform pro bono work. Besides being a mandate of the profession, providing necessary legal services for those who cannot afford them is good for business, and it's good for the soul, too.

I once handled a 94–142 case for a deaf and blind child who had been denied an appropriate education in a north Chicago suburb. When the case was finally heard by an administrative law judge, the other side, the school district, had assembled more than 30 witnesses, none of whom had actually evaluated the child, but who were ready to testify that she was hopelessly retarded, an institutional case.

Our side had the girl, her mother, a case worker/advocate, and a hearing/sight-impaired teacher who had worked with the seven-year-old.

We won, of course, and it made me more proud of being a lawyer than I had ever been before, or ever felt since, because I did it for all the right reasons. My skill and education had been used to help someone without tangible benefit to me, unless you can count the feeling I got when the mother shook my hand, tears in her eyes.

Handling pro bono work should be a requirement for every lawyer in every firm. It reminds us of what the practice of law is all about and why, when we were young and idealistic, we decided to become lawyers in the first place.

Some county bar associations honor firms and individual lawyers who devote some of their time to helping others. The law firm of Jennings, Strous & Salmon in Phoenix, Arizona, for example, was awarded Maricopa County's pro bono award for offering free services to a chain of grocery stores.

Volunteer to work on charity boards. Each year, United Way has a fund drive. So do the Red Cross, the Shriners, the Diabetes Association, Easter Seals, American Heart Association, Boy and Girl Scouts, local hospitals, and hospices: many worthwhile agencies.

The leaders in your community are often asked to chair these drives, and working to help those institutions reach their goals is a valuable use of your spare time. First, you are again doing something of value for your community. The old saw has been proven right many times: *you only get out of something what you put into it.* In this case, it's your community.

You also stand to meet the most influential people in your town, and be remembered by them as someone who is willing to work for the betterment of the community. And you stand to get some free press coverage for your efforts.

But the real reason you should help charity fund drives is because they do good things for your community, and you should support them with your time, as well as your money.

Support your alma mater. You can gain valuable exposure while supporting your college and law school by serving on any number of volunteer boards and committees. The exposure can consist of local newspaper and television coverage of events in which you are a participant and national or regional coverage in the school's alumni magazine or newsletter, as well as in the development of contacts among influential alumni/ae you meet as a result of your activities.

Homecomings are a time to rekindle old friendships, to be sure, but they should also be viewed as a way to forge new relationships with people who may be of help to your firm's future. Often, the alumni association director can be of assistance in helping you make the necessary contacts and in placing you on committees where you can rub elbows with those most like to be beneficial to your long-term plans.

Some alumni association directors of large schools have a great deal of political power because of the friendships they have developed with influential people over the years, and you should be careful to develop a relationship with them, too.

As with any other editors, the editors of the alumni magazines and newsletters are eager for information and material to place in the class notes sections, as well as for feature article ideas. But the relationship with these individuals should be cultivated as carefully as with the editors of national publications. The circulation of some of these publications may exceed 100,000 each issue, and some are distributed internationally.

One of the magazines I founded was the flagship publication of the University of Illinois, a massive, multicampus university. That publication, *Illinois Quarterly,* had a circulation of 108,000, and counted among its readers the following:

60,000 readers in Illinois, alone.

35,000 readers in metropolitan Chicago.

17,000 business, commerce, and MBA grads.

32,000 LAS grads.

7,250 educators.

6,280 agriculturalists.

2,300 attorneys.

2,000 journalists.

And 11 CEOs of Fortune 500 companies, making its readership fertile ground for almost any practice to plow.

That publication, like almost all alumni magazines and newsletters, will accept advertising at rates that may be very attractive for reaching educated audiences, especially if the school's alumni/ae are concentrated in a regional area.

You can find more information about your school's publications programs simply by calling or writing to them, or by looking in *Standard Rates & Data* or *Writer's Market* under "college and alumni publications."

Support your local sheriff. Local police officers in small towns often recommend attorneys to people they have arrested. If criminal defense work is an area of practice that interests you, maintain cordial, professional relations with your local police department.

Serve on the boards of local companies, hospitals, foundations, and similar organizations. If offered a position on the board of a local company, hospital, foundation, or similar entity, accept it gladly. Generally, there is no compensation for such an honor, but it is a mark of your acceptance as a leader in your field, and others will regard your service as an indication that you should serve on their boards, too.

As with everything else in marketing, creating the perception of quality in the minds of present and prospective clients is the most important task you face. Service on boards helps to create that perception and may bring lucrative contacts as well.

OTHER AREAS FOR COMMUNITY RELATIONS EFFORTS

Each attorney's individual areas of interest will open additional avenues for community service that can have a positive effect on his or her practice.

Each such opportunity should be evaluated with the following questions in mind, however:

- *What positive exposure can I expect to get in response to my service?*
- *What contacts can I reasonably expect to make as a result of my service?*
- *How will I be able to measure the effectiveness of my service as a marketing tool?*
- *Are there any negative exposure possibilities with respect to my service, and, if so, how can they be mitigated?*

(This last question is perhaps most appropriately asked when a decision to consider involvement in local, county, or statewide politics is made. As we all have seen, the lives of politically active individuals are subjected to the most rigorous scrutiny by the press. Therefore, any decision to enter politics should be carefully weighed and all possibilities of embarassment to the attorney and the firm should be considered.)

SAMPLE NEWS RELEASE

(Your Letterhead)

(Date)

Contact: (The name of the individual at the firm
to be contacted by editors wanting more
information)

For Immediate Release: (or for release on a
particular date)

Head: Local Law Firm to Sponsor Scholarship

(Hometown, USA) The law firm of Smith & Jones has
announced that, beginning this spring, it will
sponsor an annual scholarship for area high
school students.
 The $500 scholarship will be awarded to the
student whose essay on the subject (name the
subject) is judged best by a panel composed of
one of the partners at Smith & Jones, local

(more)

Scholarship Program

Page 2

educators, and an official from (company,
hospital, etc. that has agreed to assist and that
has an interest in the subject of the essay).
 According to John Smith, the senior partner at
Smith & Jones, the scholarship program is being
initiated to encourage scholarship and assist
students in attending the college (or nursing
school, or vocational school, etc.) of their
choice.
 ''We are very happy to be a part of this
community,'' said Smith, ''and we are very happy
to make a commitment to its future by investing
in its most valuable resource: its talented
youth.''
 The scholarship essay rules, guidelines, and
other details may be obtained from the guidance
offices of local area high schools after Monday,
(date).

(end)

Chapter Six

Become an Expert in Your Field

"An expert is one who knows more and more about less and less."

Nicholas Murray Butler (1862–1948),
President of Columbia University

People who are considered to be experts in their field weren't born that way. They became experts through formal education, disciplined self-study, voracious reading, interacting with experts who were already established, years of experience in their chosen field, publishing articles, giving seminars or lectures, and participating in associations or other groups that constantly study developments in those fields.

People who are considered to be experts are, predictably, asked for their opinions more often than those who are not experts because their opinions are regarded as having greater value than the opinions of others less qualified.

There is no easy way to become an expert in any field of law. It takes time and devotion, and some strategy and self-promotion. It is creating the perception in others of your expertise, a perception that you must then, as always, back with performance.

Typically, an attorney in private practice is not going to have the luxury of taking several years off to take a formal degree program in an area in which she or he wishes to develop specialized expertise, but there are other ways to increase knowledge and gain a reputation as an expert in any field.

FIRST, LEARN EVERYTHING YOU CAN

To gain special knowledge, there are no shortcuts. You must work hard to learn more about the field than others who work in it. It may seem an impossible task, but it's not. Like any other endeavor worth doing, it takes a pot of glue. Just smear it over the seat of your pants and sit down. Don't get up until the job is finished.

Locate the most comprehensive text in the field you wish to pursue and buy it. Then read it. Take it a chapter at a time. Take notes as you read. If you have questions, write to the author through his or her publisher. And make your own audiotapes of difficult sections so you can listen to them while you drive, walk, or jog.

The important thing is to immerse yourself in the basics of the field; when you get to the point where you are beginning to acknowledge that you don't have a grasp of areas you didn't even know existed before you started, you're well on the way to becoming well grounded. And, you will know how to keep your knowledge of case law in the area current, because you will know what to look for.

You should also determine which professional and trade publications deal with your area of interest. Your local librarian can help you find listings of such periodicals. Subscribe to them and read those, too, making note of the names of authors whose works impress you, and keep them in a card file grouped by subject matter.

Find out which societies, practice sections, and other groups there are that devote time to the study and practice of that area of the law in which you have selected to become an expert. Write to them asking for information on joining those groups, literature, and information on seminars that you might be able to attend. Join the groups, offer your services as a volunteer, and attend the seminars. Not only will you learn from others, but you will increase your network of contacts.

Don't limit yourself to law groups, practice sections, and other groups, however. You may find that lawyers who are truly expert in a field may belong to engineering societies, for example, or journalism societies, and not-for-profit entities, depending upon their areas of concentration. Sometimes the names of such people are listed in regional and national editions of *Who's Who.*

Lawyers I knew who were involved in aviation accident litigation frequently belonged to such organizations as the Helicopter Association of America and the Air Line Pilots' Association, and developed relationships with investigators employed by the Federal Aviation Administration, the National Transportation Safety Board, and state agencies. They also subscribed to, and got to know the editors of magazines that were read by pilots, such as *Rotor & Wing* and *Private Pilot.* Much of their knowledge was obtained by osmosis—simply by surrounding themselves with people who were experts themselves.

You should also take both law and nonlaw related courses to enrich your knowledge of the area and to give you credibility in the field. A practitioner who is interested in becoming an expert in the field of aviation accident litigation might be well advised to take courses on metallurgy, accident investigation, and aeronautical engineering, for example. Another, bent on gaining a reputation in the field of medical malpractice litigation, might benefit from taking courses in nursing, anatomy, or hospital administration.

Make a list of those people you regard as experts in the field. If possible, develop relationships with them, and find out not only how they became so accomplished in their fields, but why. (Sometimes the why is more important than the how, because it gives insight into the personality traits that may be required to function as an expert in the field.) Then emulate the ways in which they gained their expertise and obtained their reputation.

There are countless ways in which you can develop a firm foundation in the body of knowledge necessary to make you an expert in your field. You are limited only by your imagination in your quest to learn everything that you can on the subject you have selected.

ESTABLISH A DAILY REGIMEN FOR SELF-IMPROVEMENT

Just as you have a daily regimen for eating, for exercising, for going to work, and other matters, you need to develop a daily regimen for acquiring new expertise. It should be no less than an hour a day, and it should be the same hour each day, so that eventually the time devoted to study will become a lifelong habit of learning.

If you feel that there just aren't enough hours in each day to devote one to self-improvement, try this exercise: for two weeks, keep track of every minute of nonbillable time you spend at the office, whether it's reading the newspaper, taking an extra half-hour for lunch, daydreaming, shopping on company time, whatever. At the end of the period, add up the time that was spent on nonproductive pursuits. You will find that there is more than enough time to devote to increasing your knowledge in your field.

Once you have established a daily regimen, you must stick to it, the way an athlete must constantly train to meet his or her goals. The temptation to take a few days off is great, but it may cost you your goal. Keep the pot of glue handy.

GAIN EXPERIENCE IN THE FIELD

To gain experience, volunteer to do pro bono work if it's available in the field. In many areas, court appointments are available to represent the indigent, children, and others as guardian ad litem in a variety of matters, and there is often the opportunity to represent criminal defendants as a part-time public defender, if criminal work is something you relish.

To gain experience in handling cases involving abused and handicapped children, I once volunteered to act as guardian ad litem for a child who had been the subject of physical, as well as sexual abuse. I found the rewards of that representation so great that I went on to serve as counsel to the county's multidisciplinary team on child abuse. Although I will not say that I became an expert in the field, I did learn a great deal about the processes involved, particularly the machinations of the agencies, that, once mastered, made practice in the area much easier and efficient. And, I had a number of such cases referred to me in the years that followed, many from social workers I had met in my official capacities.

You may also gain experience by volunteering to assist a senior attorney who is an expert in the area in which you wish to become more knowledgeable. Offer to do it for free, to learn the ropes. The education you receive will be priceless, and you will also become associated in the minds of others with that attorney.

And, you should take cases on referral in the area, despite the inability of the individual to pay what you would normally charge. Again, you are obtaining an education.

PUBLISH IN YOUR FIELD

There is probably no greater, single learning experience than writing an article for publication. The research and concentration that are required to create a publishable piece will add to your growing body of knowledge, and people who read the articles you write will begin to associate your name with the field.

If you are not a polished writer, there is no shame in asking an accomplished editor to help you prepare a manuscript for submission. Most competent editors will charge somewhere between $25 to $50 an hour, more for technical pieces, to help you "massage" your article into final form. Choose the editor based upon his or her experience in developing articles for the type of publication to which you are seeking to submit your work. Each genre is different, and requires different styles.

Don't limit yourself to writing law review–style articles. If the people you wish to present yourself to as an expert are blue collar factory workers, you'll have a better chance of reaching them by writing a piece for the local daily or for their company's house organ. If I were interested in obtaining a national reputation for domestic relations work, I might consider writing articles for such publications as *Redbook* or *Parents Magazine.*

Similarly, if your target is a company president, the trade and business magazines he or she subscribes to are apt choices for submitting articles tailored to their styles. If the companies are small or family-owned entities, *Nation's Business* would be a likely periodical to target with information-rich, how-to articles.

Most editors will provide you with their editorial guidelines for a self-addressed, stamped envelope. And, you can use the *Writer's Market* (Writer's Digest Books) at your local library to discover what trade and association periodicals there are in your field. *Writer's Market* will also often include the readership of a listed publication.

I started writing for pleasure while actively practicing law. My first piece was a short article for *Parents Magazine* about a sleep-out my then-five-year-old son and I shared. Since then, writing and editing have grown to be my primary means of earning a living. I have written for a number of national consumer, trade, business, professional, and scholarly publications. I used *Writer's Market* in the beginning to find markets for my work, and I still do.

If you do publish an article or two for a periodical in the field you've chosen, be careful to cultivate the relationship you are developing with the editor with whom you work. Editors can assign work to writers, and are also often used as a resource by people in the field looking for speakers, writers, and lecturers. If the editor believes in you and your knowledge, if you deliver top-notch work *on time,* and if you are pleasant to work with, that editor could well become one of your biggest cheerleaders and advocates. I think it was my father who told me that if a man tells you he is very good at his trade, take it with a grain of salt. But if another tradesman compliments a man's work, chances are he is very good.

WRITE A BOOK

·If you have the time and the energy to write a book, go ahead. If you're a plaintiff's attorney, you can rapidly gain a national reputation in your field by writing a book and getting on the talk show circuit. But such book success stories are rare, and, when they do occur, it is often the individual's reputation *before* publication that got the book published in the first place.

Beware of vanity presses which will publish your manuscript, so long as you pay for it. If reputable publishing houses won't accept your manuscript for publication, it doesn't mean it's not good. It may mean that, in their experience, the topic will not sell well enough for them to cover their costs and make a profit.

Still, there are reasons for self-publishing. If your target audience is very small and specialized, for example, no publisher may want to produce a book in such limited numbers, despite the quality of the research and writing. In such a case, self-publication may be the only way in which to get the book into print.

Having a professional author ghostwrite a book for you, particularly a book aimed at a general audience, is a time-saving, but expensive alternative to writing a book yourself. According to the 1993 *Writer's Market,* the fees may be as high as $35,000.

If you contemplate writing a book on a case that you have been involved in, make sure that all your dealings with your client are at arm's length, meet ethical guidelines, *and that you protect your client's interests.* Your book may be successful, but if you are seen as parlaying your position of trust into an opportunity to profit from the adversity of another, you will never be trusted again.

You should also protect yourself by having any agreements with the client in writing, and encourage the client to engage independent counsel.

Before You Write That Book or Article . . .

Before you go to the trouble of writing an article or book for publication, send written queries to editors to see if they would be interested in an article on topics you suggest. Most editors receive far more unsolicited manuscripts than they can deal with; many are returned unopened, and some are simply thrown away.

An effective query letter should spark the editor's interest and, if he or she is interested in seeing more, you will be contacted to discuss the matter further.

I usually enclose a postcard with my query letters, asking editors to check whether they are interested or not in the proposed article. I always get a response that way.

There are as many opinions as to what makes a good query letter as there are writers, but in general, a query should quickly and concisely tell the editor what the story line is, why it is topical, and why his readers would want to read it. I sometimes also include a sample lead paragraph for the proposed article to demonstrate how the reader will be lured into reading the entire piece. And I also enclose clips of my published works to indicate that I have the requisite skills to complete the assignment, should the work be commissioned.

If you don't have clips, enclose a resume. Your professional qualifications to write the article are every bit as important as your writing ability. An editor can, and often does, change wording and style to suit his readership, but does not have the time to do legal research.

TEACH AS MUCH AS POSSIBLE

Accept each and every opportunity you are offered to teach a course in your field, give a lecture, or act as a guest speaker. The more you speak, the more you will be asked to speak. And the more you teach, the greater the number of students who will go forth believing that you are the guru in your field.

Like writing, teaching and lecturing are also great learning opportunities for you, and not just because you must prepare for the class or presentation. You will learn from the questions that are asked and the comments that are made by students and members of the audience.

I once thought I knew a great deal about business law. I had taught a CPA review course at night (three hours, once a week, with one 10-minute break). Then I was asked to substitute at a local college as an adjunct professor of business law for a semester.

In retrospect, I realized that I had prepared poorly for the first class. I underestimated the students' desire to learn and their own experiences.

The questions they asked were probing, intelligent ones that often I could not answer as glibly as I expected to be able to. As a result, I prepared for the remaining classes that semester as though I were preparing to take the bar exam again.

By teaching business law that semester, I learned more about the UCC than I had during law school. It increased my body of knowledge in a way that studying alone never could have accomplished.

I felt the same way when I was asked to address a graduating nursing class on potential professional liability matters. That led to an address before seniors in a small college who were studying to become registered dietitians. I learned not only by preparing, but by the interaction with the students.

You will also find that by teaching you will become more of a teacher in the office, too, both with your staff and your clients. You will find that you are more interested in making sure that you are understood than in issuing orders. Ask your secretary if she would like that.

SEEK PROFESSIONAL LICENSES

If experts in the field you have chosen to study typically have a professional license, such as certification as a public accountant or financial planner, a pilot's license, a real estate broker's license, an SEC license, or similar certifications, make the effort to obtain it. You will learn more about the field by studying for the examination and you will also gain credibility with others because of the license you have earned. Don't confuse this with the Scarecrow in the Wizard of Oz getting his diploma; you should take the requisite courses from approved institutions and pass the exam in order to gain knowledge. The credibility is the dessert, not the object, of the exercise, yet the credibility can be of utmost importance in some cases.

Once I had the opportunity to take the pretrial deposition of the opposing expert in a medical malpractice case. The case had to do with injuries a prematurely delivered infant suffered during and immediately after birth. My expert was a board-certified neonatologist, a doctor who specialized in the care and treatment of the newborn.

The opposing expert, I learned during the deposition, had taken the board examinations for certification in neonatology, but had failed them. His credibility as an expert, of course, was demolished by that realization. The case settled within hours after the deposition was concluded.

MAKE YOUR EXPERTISE KNOWN

Let people in the community and the press know that you have expertise in a narrow area of the law, but do it carefully, so that it doesn't seem like you're being too self-promoting.

A news release to trade publications and newspapers upon your being conferred a new degree or being granted a license is appropriate. If you have a brochure that you use to introduce prospective clients to your firm, include the special training and abilities that might well separate your firm from others seeking the same work.

If possible, develop a relationship with reporters who cover special beats where your skill and knowledge might be valuable to them as a quotable source. Being treated by the press as an expert will create that perception in the mind of those who read the articles.

NEVER STOP LEARNING

Perhaps the best advice anyone could give on how to become an expert on practically anything is to never stop searching for knowledge, never discount any source as a possible source of information, and always look for ways in which your knowledge will be tested by interaction with others.

You will never learn it all; you can only hope to learn enough to know what it is you do not yet know. Like the search for quality, the search for knowledge is a never-ending one.

Chapter Seven

Advertising

THE PURPOSES OF ADVERTISING

The purposes of advertising are to inform, to persuade, and to create a perception of quality and value. How those things are done depends in large measure upon the audience you seek to inform, what it is you wish to persuade them to do, and how they may individually define quality and value.

A corporate CEO may define quality and value as obtaining a desired result within a preset budget for legal services. To persuade that CEO, you may have to inform him or her of the quality of services you have provided others similarly situated and the expertise of the attorneys on staff who would be assigned to that company's cases, and inform him or her that you are willing to enter into win-win fee arrangements.

An unemployed, injured man may define quality as a free consultation regarding the likelihood of his recovering damages for his injuries without having to pay anything out of pocket until the matter is settled. Advertising on television that your firm provides free, initial consultations and that your firm accepts cases on a contingency fee basis may prompt that person to contact your office, if such ads are permitted within your jurisdiction.

In an episode of the old Dick Van Dyke Show, "Rob" invests in a shoe store and, upset that the salesman is treating the customers rudely, takes over the job of selling discount footwear. He sells a few pair, but his record cannot compare to that of the surly employee.

The manager of the store then explains to Rob that the customers expect to be treated rudely, that they associate that treatment with low prices and bargains. In effect, if the customers were treated nicely, the manager says, they would feel as though they were paying too much for the shoes.

What Rob learned was that the secret to selling shoes was nothing more than discovering, and satisfying, the perception of quality that the potential customer had. It's no different in using advertising to sell legal services.

THE TYPES OF ADVERTISING

It was not that many years ago that lawyers did not advertise, either because of restrictions imposed by their states' rules governing professional conduct, or because it was regarded as unprofessional. Now most do. According to a survey conducted by *Of Counsel* magazine, 66.2 percent of the 146 firms responding stated that they place ads of one sort or another other than "tombstone" ads. And they use a variety of media to advertise their services.

Word of mouth.   The best form of advertising is word of mouth, and chances are you have already enjoyed the benefit of personal referrals from people for whom you have obtained good results in the past. By seeking to provide clients with the highest quality of legal services, and by treating them with the respect they deserve, you will continue to receive such referrals.

Each person in your office should be aware that how they conduct themselves, both on and off the job, can have a positive impact upon how the firm is viewed, and how the firm will be discussed by others.

Print advertising.   Print advertising is primarily found in newspapers and magazines. It is either display advertising (e.g., full-page ads, quarter-page ads, etc.) or classified advertising. To be effective, print advertising must be placed in publications that the target audience reads. It may or may not involve the use of a reply card that recipients can use to request additional information.

Directory advertising.   As the name implies, directory advertising involves the use of directories—the Yellow Pages, Martindale-Hubbel, business-to-business directories, annual trade directories, and so forth, to inform others of the services your firm offers.

Direct mail advertising.   Sometimes called "junk mail," direct mail is a very effective way to reach large numbers of people who share demographic characteristics that advertisers find attractive. Their names and addresses are obtained from lists that are sold or rented from list brokers. (In *Zauderer* v. *Office of Disciplinary Counsel of the Supreme Court of Ohio,* 471 U.S. 627 [1985], the Supreme Court ruled that a state cannot prohibit lawyers from using direct mail advertising that is not false or misleading.)

Electronic advertising.   Electronic advertising includes the purchase of radio and television time and, more recently, the use of computer-based bread board systems ("BBS" or "bulletin boards"), and even rental videocassettes to carry messages. In using electronic bulletin boards, lawyers should be careful that they do not engage in the unauthorized practice of law by giving advice to persons whose problems arise in jurisdictions in which the lawyer is not admitted. (See, for example, an article that I wrote for the June 1993 issue of the *ABA Journal,* entitled, "PC Practitioners Proliferate.") Also, lawyers who are admitted in more than one jurisdiction should ensure that advertising that may be heard or viewed by potential clients in each of those jurisdictions will not violate the disciplinary rules of either.

Telemarketing.   Telemarketing is the use of telephones to take surveys or solicit business. It may also involve the use of fax machines to reach large numbers in a relatively inexpensive manner. In this endeavor, as in the use of direct mail, the development of the list of persons to be contacted is most important.

Outdoor and transit advertising.   Outdoor advertising is the use of billboards and signs. Transit advertising is the use of space on or inside trains, buses, taxis, and other forms of mass transit.

Other forms of advertising.   Placing information on articles of clothing, imprinting your firm's name on calendars or other freebies that are distributed to present and prospective clients (if allowed in your jurisdiction), using skywriters, having a message or product appear in motion pictures or on the screens of local theaters before the feature presentation—any form of mass paid communication is advertising.

THE ETHICS OF LAWYER ADVERTISING

Bates v. State Bar of Arizona, 433 U.S. 350 (1977).   In 1977, the Supreme Court held blanket prohibitions against lawyer advertising unconstitutional, but permitted regulation to some degree.

The Court's decision in *Bates* only went so far as to say that the states could prevent "false, deceptive or misleading advertising" and that "We expect that the bar will have a special role to play in assuring that advertising by attorneys flows both freely and cleanly." 433 U.S. 350, 384.

That last statement was interpreted by some states to impose harsh restrictions on attorney advertising. As those rules were challenged, the Court removed barrier after barrier until now, except in a few jurisdictions, the only remaining prohibitions are against "false, deceptive and misleading" advertising and, where applicable, in-person or live telephone solicitations.

The ABA Model Rules.   The ABA Model Rules of Professional Conduct permit advertising "through public media, such as a telephone directory, legal directory, newspaper or other periodical, outdoor advertising, radio or television, or through written or recorded communication," as long as the lawyer keeps a copy or recording of the communication, and a record of how it was disseminated, for at least two years after its last use. The ads used must also include the name of at least one attorney responsible for its content. (Rule 7.2)

The Model Rules prohibit "in-person or live telephone" solicitations for "professional employment from a prospective client with whom the lawyer has no family or prior professional relationship when a significant motive for the lawyer's doing so is the lawyer's pecuniary gain." But the rules do permit the use of direct mail, unless the prospective client has made it known that he does not want to receive such solicitations, provided the lawyer clearly marks the envelope and contents of the mailing as "Advertising Material." (Rule 7.3)

State rules.   The Model Rules, however, have not been adopted blindly by the states. Though the comment to Model Rule 7.2 states that "prohibiting television advertising . . . would impede the flow of information about legal services to many sectors of the public," some jurisdictions have adopted tough policies prohibiting television ads as well as ads thought to be "undignified."

In Florida, for example, attorneys using the television as an advertising medium are forbidden to use dramatic scenes, slogans, endorsements from clients, celebrity voices or endorsements, any background sound other than instrumental music, or moving pictures. Their TV ads must also be accompanied by a disclaimer which states that "The hiring of a lawyer is an important decision that should not be based solely upon advertisements. Before you decide, ask us to send you free written information about our qualifications and experience."

Other states that have adopted regulations more stringent than those in the ABA Model Rules include the following.

Alabama.   "No communication concerning a lawyer's services shall be published or broadcast unless it contains the following language, which shall be clearly legible or audible, as the case may be: No representation is made that the quality of the legal services to be performed is greater than the quality of legal services performed by other lawyers." (Rule 7.2)

Alaska.   DR 2–101 sets forth a list of the 25 permissible types of information that a lawyer may use in an advertisement. It also provides that a lawyer may make application to the Alaska Bar Association for permission to add other information. No direct mail solicitation is permitted. However, the Supreme Court expressly ruled in *Shapero* v. *Kentucky Bar Association,* 486 U.S. 466 (1988) that targeted direct mail solicitation is protected as commercial free speech under the First Amendment. Also excluded by Alaska rules are "self-laudatory" statements.

Arizona.   Direct mail solicitations must have the following notice, printed in red ink, all capitals, at least double the type size used in the body text, on the envelope and first page of the written communication: ADVERTISING MATERIAL: THIS COMMERCIAL SOLICITATION HAS NOT BEEN APPROVED BY THE STATE BAR OF ARIZONA.

Arkansas.   Direct-mail pieces must be clearly marked "advertising" and copies must be maintained by the lawyer distributing them for at least five years.

California.   Communications that contain a testimonial must also contain the following disclaimer: "This testimonial or endorsement does not constitute a guarantee, warranty, or prediction regarding the outcome of your legal matter." Prohibited: "Communications" transmitted at the scene of an accident or at or en route to a hospital, emergency care center, or other health care facility.

Colorado. Copies of print ads and recordings of television or radio ads must be kept for three years. Direct-mail lists should also be maintained for three years.

Connecticut. Personal or live telephone contact, including telemarketing contact, with prospective clients is permitted in the following circumstances: 1. If the prospective client is a close friend, relative, former client or one whom the lawyer reasonably believes to be a client; 2. Under the auspices of a public or charitable legal services organization; 3. Under the auspices of a bona fide political, social, civic, fraternal, employee, or trade association whose purposes include but are not limited to the principal purposes of the organization; or 4. If the prospective client is a business organization, a not-for-profit organization, or governmental body and the lawyer seeks to provide services related to the organization.

Delaware. If a lawyer lists the areas in which he or she concentrates, the following disclaimer must be made: "Listing of areas of practice does not represent official certification as a specialist in those areas." When a specific fee, magnitude of fee, or range of fee is advertised, the lawyer must identify with particularity the specific service(s) to which the fee information applies, must state that costs and disbursements are not included, if that is the case, and state that "The extent of legal services required depends upon the facts in each case. If additional services are required, full information on additional charges will be provided at the first consultation."

District of Columbia. "No lawyer or any person acting on behalf of a lawyer shall solicit or invite or seek to solicit any person for purposes of representing that person for a fee paid by or on behalf of a client or under the Criminal Justice Act, D.C. Code Ann. 11–2601 et seq., in any present or future case in the District of Columbia courthouse, on the sidewalks of the north, south and west sides of the courthouse, or within 50 feet of the building on the east side."

Florida. In addition to the restrictions on television advertising set forth earlier in this chapter, all ads must specify the geographic location of the office in which the lawyer(s) who will actually perform the services advertised principally practice law. Any lawyer who advertises must have available in printed form for delivery to any potential client the following information: 1. A factual statement detailing the background, training, and experience of each lawyer in the firm. 2. If the lawyer or law firm claims special expertise in the representation of clients in special matters or publicly limits the lawyer's or law firm's practice to special types of cases or clients, the written information shall set forth the factual details of the lawyer's experience, expertise, background, and training in such matters.

A 30-day "cooling off" period is required to be observed before an attorney may contact a potential client when the communication relates to a personal injury or wrongful death claim or an accident or disaster.

And, copies of ads, with some exceptions, must be filed with the Florida Bar together with a fee of $25.

Georgia.   Any ad that contains information concerning contingent fees must also state that "Contingent attorneys' fees refers only to those fees charged by attorneys for their legal services. Such fees are not permitted in all types of cases. Court costs and other additional expenses of legal actions usually must be paid by the client." In addition, any communication that contains the phrase "No fee unless you win or collect," or similar language, must also contain the following disclaimer: " 'No fee unless you win or collect' refers only to fees charged by the attorney. Such contingent fees are not permitted in all types of cases. Court costs and other additional expenses of legal action usually must be paid by the client."

Direct mail is permitted, but not if it is prompted by a specific occurrence related to the recipient or a member of his or her family and which could give rise to an action for personal injury or wrongful death.

Hawaii.   Sample copies of all direct mail pieces must be sent to the state's Office of Disciplinary Counsel.

Idaho.   No significant differences.

Illinois.   Telephone contact solicitation is permitted if the potential client is a relative, a close friend, or a person with whom the lawyer or the lawyer's firm has had a prior professional relationship, or under the auspices of a public or charitable legal services organization, or a bona fide political, social, civic, charitable, religious, fraternal, employee, or trade organization whose purposes include but are not limited to providing or recommending legal services.

Iowa.   All disclaimers required by Iowa rules must be printed in type no smaller than 9 point. General print advertising may be published only in the geographic area in which the lawyer maintains offices or in which a significant part of the lawyer's clientele resides. No "unrestrained subjective characterizations of rates or fees, such as but not limited to, 'cut-rate,' 'lowest,' 'give-away,' 'below-cost,' 'discount,' and 'special.'" No in-person or telephone solicitations of any kind. Prior filing with the Iowa State Bar Association of all direct mail pieces; approval is required before mailing. Direct mailings must go to the general public and not targeted groups. Television and radio ads can have a single "nondramatic" voice, not that of the lawyer, with no other background sound. In the case of television, there is no visual display allowed other than that allowed in print as articulated by the announcer. Radio and television ads, to the extent possible, must be broadcast only in the geographical area in which the lawyer maintains offices or in which a significant part of the lawyer's clientele resides. Lawyers who quote fixed fees for specific legal services are limited to 12 areas in which such fees may be stated as fixed, including uncontested dissolutions of marriage involving no disagreement concerning custody of children, alimony, child support, or property settlement.

Kansas.   No significant differences.

Kentucky.   Copies of all print ads and cassette recordings of radio and television ads must be filed with the Attorneys Advertising Commission. Statements concerning contingent fees must include "plus court costs." Statements to the effect that an attorney will perform a routine service for a stated fee must file with the commission and give to each prospective client a detailed definition of what services are included. Any advertisements that list or suggest areas of an attorney's practice must state the following: "This is an advertisement. Kentucky law does not certify specialties of legàl practice."

Louisiana.   Direct mail pieces must be identified as such on the envelope and first page in type twice as large as the type otherwise appearing on the envelope or page. All direct-mail pieces must be filed with the State Bar Association.

Maine.   No significant differences.

Maryland. Telephone contact solicitation is permitted if the potential client is a relative, a close friend, or a person with whom the lawyer or the lawyer's firm has had a prior professional relationship, or is under the auspices of a public or charitable legal services organization or a bona fide political, social, civic, charitable, religious, fraternal, employee, or trade organization whose purposes include but are not limited to providing or recommending legal services.

Massachusetts. A lawyer shall not solicit professional employment for a fee from a prospective client by written communication, audio- or videocassette, or other electronic materials, directed to such prospective clients unless each such communication is clearly labeled "advertising" on its face and on any envelope or container.

Michigan. Lawyers are not allowed to solicit professional employment from prospective clients with whom the lawyer has no family or prior professional relationship, when a significant motive for the lawyer's doing so is the lawyer's pecuniary gain, but the rule defines "solicit" in the context of *Shapero:* "[T]he term 'solicit' [does not] include 'sending truthful and nondeceptive letters to potential clients known to face particular legal problems.'"

Minnesota. No solicitations permitted in person or by telephone.

Mississippi. Copies of all advertising or written communications are required to be kept for six years. Advertised fixed fees must be accompanied by the following disclaimer: "The Rules of Professional Conduct of the Mississippi State Bar require that the above service be performed by this lawyer (or firm) for not more than the advertised fee." Soliciting is prohibited but, as in Michigan, advertising circulars and letters of the direct mail variety approved in *Shapero* are permitted. Lawyers certified by the National Board of Trial Advocacy as Board Certified Civil Trial Advocacy Specialists or Criminal Trial Advocacy Specialists may *not* advertise those designations. Statements such as "No fee will be charged until your case is won" were found to be in violation of this state's professional conduct rules because they "may prompt an unjustified expectation that the lawyer is exceptionally successful in winning his or her cases." (Ethics Committee of the Mississippi State Bar Opinion No. 163, June 23, 1989)

Missouri. A communication is regarded as false or misleading if it contains any paid testimonial about or paid endorsement of the lawyer, without identifying the fact that payment has been made, or, if the testimonial or endorsement is not made by an actual client, without identifying that fact. Also, any simulated description, visualization, or representation of the lawyer, his partners or associates, his offices or facilities, or his services without identifying the fact that the description is a simulation is also regarded as false or misleading. Telephone contact solicitation is permitted if the potential client is a relative, a close friend, or a person with whom the lawyer or the lawyer's firm has had a prior professional relationship, or is under the auspices of a public or charitable legal services organization, or a bona fide political, social, civic, charitable, religious, fraternal, employee, or trade organization whose purposes include but are not limited to providing or recommending legal services.

Montana. No significant differences.

Nebraska. If a lawyer publishes fee information in a publication that has no fixed date for publication of a succeeding issue, the lawyer shall be bound by any representation made therein for a reasonable period of time after publication but in no event less than one year. Telephone contact solicitation is permitted if the potential client is a relative, a close friend, or a person with whom the lawyer or the lawyer's firm has had a prior professional relationship, or is under the auspices of a public or charitable legal services organization or a bona fide political, social, civic, charitable, religious, fraternal, employee, or trade organization whose purposes include but are not limited to providing or recommending legal services.

Nevada. Lawyers may advertise that they limit their practice to three of the 36 listed areas of concentration. The following disclaimer is then required: "Neither the State Bar of Nevada nor any agency of the State Bar has certified any lawyer identified here as a specialist or as an expert. Anyone considering a lawyer should independently investigate the lawyer's credentials and ability." Lawyers who wish to communicate that they limit their practice must certify that they have done the following each calendar year: devoted at least 300 hours each year to each separate designated field of practice for each of the preceding two calendar years; completed six hours of accredited continuing legal education in each designated field of the practice during the preceding calendar year. The name of a deceased partner may be used by a firm on stationery, window lettering, business cards, and legal directories for a period not to exceed three years.

New Hampshire. Soliciting is prohibited but, as in Michigan, advertising circulars and letters of the direct mail variety approved in *Shapero* are permitted.

New Jersey. "All advertisements shall be presented in a dignified manner without the use of drawings, animations, dramatization, music, or lyrics." Direct-mail pieces must have the following disclaimer: "Before making your choice of attorney, you should give this matter careful thought. The selection of an attorney is an important decision," and a notice that the recipient may, if he or she regards the mailing to be inaccurate or misleading, report it to the Committee on Attorney Advertising, together with that committee's address.

New Mexico. Lawyers may not list their names in directories under headings such as "Lawyers—Grouped by Type of Practice" for a particular area of law in which the state's supreme court has established a specialization program unless they are registered specialists in that area.

New York. New York's rules prohibit puffery, self-laudation, claims regarding the quality of the lawyer's legal services, or any other claims that cannot be measured or verified. Advertisers who publish statements concerning fixed fees for certain services are required to list, in detail, the nature of the services to be provided and must provide prospective clients with a copy at the time they are retained. Lawyers are bound to provide services for fees stated in broadcast advertisements for a period of not less than 30 days. For fees advertised in periodicals, the period is not less than 30 days if the newspaper or magazine is published more frequently than once per month, until the next issue is published if the frequency is once per month or less often, and, in the case of publications which have no fixed publication schedule, a reasonable period of time not less than 90 days. Only lawyers certified by the state as specialists may hold themselves out as such. Copies of all advertisements must be filed with the Departmental Disciplinary Committee, and, if the advertisement is a direct-mail piece, the mailing list must be retained for at least one year.

North Carolina. Firms maintaining offices in the state may not list the names of attorneys who are not licensed to practice in North Carolina as attorneys affiliated with the firm. Firms that practice in more than one jurisdiction must identify in their communications the jurisdictional limitations of those not licensed in North Carolina. No attorney may maintain a permanent professional relationship with a lawyer not licensed to practice in North Carolina unless offices are maintained in the state and in a state in which the lawyer is licensed and a registration certificate authorizing the relationship is obtained from the State Bar. Limitation of practice areas in communications must bear the following notice: "Representations of specialty do not indicate state certification of expertise" unless the individual is certified as a specialist by the State Bar.

North Dakota. There are no restrictions other than the prohibitions against false and misleading statements and in-person contact.

Ohio. Lawyers are bound by fixed fees advertised in periodicals for a period of 30 days if the periodical is published more frequently than one time per month, until the date of the succeeding issue if published once a month or less frequently, and for a reasonable time, not less than one year, for publications that have no fixed date for a succeeding issue. Lawyers who are engaged in another business may not so indicate on his or her card, sign, or letterhead, nor shall he or she identify himself or herself as a lawyer in connection with his other profession or business, although the degree or title may be used. Lawyers are free to write for publication and speak publicly on legal topics so long as they do not emphasize their own professional experience or reputation and do not undertake to provide individual advice. Advertisements containing client testimonials are not permitted, according to Board of Commissioners on Grievances and Discipline Opinion 89–24, August 18, 1989. The rationale is that testimonials are subjective statements regarding the quality of a lawyer's services which cannot be verified by reference to objective standards established by the profession. Additionally, lawyers cannot avoid the ban on self-laudatory statements by having a client do so on his or her behalf. Lawyers who advertise that they handle certain types of cases must, in fact, handle those kinds of cases, and not merely refer them to other lawyers. Opinion 88–28.

Oklahoma. Direct mailings must contain the following statement: "If you find anything in this communication to be inaccurate or misleading, you may report the same by writing to the General Counsel of the Oklahoma Bar Association, P.O. Box 53036, Oklahoma City, Oklahoma 73152, or by calling 1–800–522–8065." Additionally, written communications soliciting employment must be clearly labelled as "advertisements." No certified or registered mail or other forms of restricted delivery may be used for advertising purposes. Any advertisements containing fee information must state that the client is responsible for the expenses of litigation and describe whether any contingent fee advertised is determined before or after the deduction of costs and expenses. Lawyers are bound by fixed fees advertised in periodicals for a period of 30 days if the periodical is published more frequently than one time per month, until the date of the succeeding issue if published once a month or less frequently, and for a reasonable time, not less than one year, for publications that have no fixed date for a succeeding issue. Lawyers are bound by fees advertised in mailings for six months.

Oregon. Copies of all advertisements, along with a record of when and where they were used, must be retained for a period of one year. Ads, other than direct-mail ads, must be clearly identified as such unless it is apparent from the context that they are paid advertisements. Direct-mail pieces must be identified as advertisements in all cases. Telephone contact solicitation is permitted if the potential client is a relative, a close friend, or a person with whom the lawyer or the lawyer's firm has had a prior professional relationship, or is under the auspices of a public or charitable legal services organization, or a bona fide political, social, civic, charitable, religious, fraternal, employee, or trade organization whose purposes include but are not limited to providing or recommending legal services, if the legal services are related to the principal purposes of the organization. Formal Ethics Opinion No. 520, August 1988, permits lawyers to send a letter or pamphlet inviting recipients (selected from newspaper accounts of accidents) to call and schedule a consultation to discuss possible claims.

Pennsylvania. There are no substantial differences between Pennsylvania's rules and those of the ABA Model Rules. The Committee on Legal Ethics and Professional Responsibility Opinion No. 88–241, however, states that the following terms may not be used in advertisements because they are inherently misleading: "experience," "expert," "highly qualified," and "competent."

Puerto Rico. "A lawyer who, for profit, gives unsolicited counseling or advice, encourages or promotes, in any manner, potential clients to bring lawsuits or any other types of claims, is acting against the high postulates of the profession." As may be surmised, advertising of any sort is frowned upon, including the following "inappropriate" types of advertising that include: diagrams, drawings, photographs, or any other type of illustration; self-laudatory comments or references to the quality of a lawyer's services; or claims of special expertise in any area of the law.

Rhode Island. Copies of direct-mail pieces, and listings of the individuals to whom they are sent, must be filed with the Supreme Court Disciplinary Counsel and retained by the lawyer for three years.

South Carolina. Advertisements and direct-mail pieces must be clearly labeled as advertising and include the following statements: 1. "You may wish to consult your lawyer or another lawyer instead of me (us). You may obtain information about other lawyers by consulting the Yellow Pages or by calling the South Carolina Bar Lawyer Referral Service at 799–7100 in Columbia or toll free 1–800–868–2284. If you have already engaged a lawyer in connection with the legal matter referred to in this letter, you should direct any questions you have to that lawyer;" 2. "The exact nature of your legal situation will depend on many facts not known by me (us) at this time. You should understand that the advice and information in this letter is general and that your situation may vary;" and 3. in all capital letters, "ANY COMPLAINTS ABOUT THIS LETTER (OR RECORDING) OR THE REPRESENTATION OF ANY LAWYER MAY BE DIRECTED TO THE BOARD OF COMMISSIONERS ON GRIEVANCES AND DISCIPLINE, POST OFFICE BOX 11330, COLUMBIA SOUTH CAROLINA 29211—TELEPHONE NUMBER 803–734–1150. Copies of all written or recorded communications must be filed with the board of Commissioners within 10 days together with a fee of $10. Lawyers who use written or record solicitations are required to keep a file showing the following: 1. The basis by which the lawyer knows that the person solicited needs legal services; and 2. The factual basis for any statements made in any written or recorded solicitations.

South Dakota. Direct contact solicitation, in person, by mail, or otherwise, where a significant motive for the lawyer's doing so is pecuniary gain, is prohibited, when it is targeted to a specific recipient.

Tennessee. Any communication that contains any listing of legal services for specific areas of practice must include the following statement: "Tennessee does not certify specialists in the law, and we do not claim certification in any listed area." Copies of all communications must be filed with the Board of Professional Responsibility together with a statement as to where and how it was published or broadcast. Lawyers are bound by statements concerning fees for 60 days after publication or broadcast. All communications soliciting professional employment must be clearly marked "This is an advertisement," and, in the case of video communications, the required wording "shall appear in the video portion in print size at least equivalent to the largest print used elsewhere in the communication for at least five (5) seconds duration at the beginning and five (5) seconds duration at the end of the communication." For audio communications, such as radio advertisements, the required wording must be in the same tone, speed of delivery, and clarity of the audio in the remainder of the advertisement.

Texas. There are no significant differences between Texas' rules and the ABA Model Rules.

Utah. There are no significant differences between Utah's rules and the ABA Model Rules.

Vermont. There are no significant differences between Vermont's rules and the ABA Model Rules.

Virginia. Lawyers are prohibited from initiating in-person solicitation of professional employment for compensation in a personal injury or wrongful death claim of a prospective client with whom the lawyer has no family or prior professional relationship. In-person solicitation is defined as face-to-face communication and telephone communication.

Washington. Copies of advertisements and written solicitation materials must be kept for two years together with a record of when and where they were used.

West Virginia. Copies of advertisements and written solicitation materials must be kept for two years together with a record of when and where they were used.

Wisconsin. No paid testimonials are permitted unless the fact that payment has been made is identified or, if the testimonial or endorsement is not made by an actual client, without identifying that fact. Copies of advertisements and written solicitation materials must be kept for two years together with a record of when and where they were used. Direct mail is permitted to prospective clients known to need legal services, but must be labeled as advertising. Copies must be filed with the Board of Attorneys' Professional Responsibility office. Telephone contact solicitation is permitted if the potential client is a relative, a close friend, or a person with whom the lawyer or the lawyer's firm has had a prior professional relationship, or is under the auspices of a public or charitable legal services organization, or a bona fide political, social, civic, charitable, religious, fraternal, employee, or trade organization whose purposes include but are not limited to providing or recommending legal services, if the legal services are related to the principal purposes of the organization.

Wyoming. There are no significant differences between Wyoming's rules and the ABA Model Rules.

Note: The above are examples of portions of state rules dealing with publicity and advertising. They are not meant to be all-inclusive. Check your state's rules and the opinions issued by its board charged with the duty of interpreting them before you engage in any marketing activities.

MEASURING THE EFFECTIVENESS OF YOUR ADVERTISING

The effectiveness of your advertising program can be measured as inexpensively as asking clients how they learned of your services or as complex as engaging an advertising agency to build in tracking systems for each ad.

To ensure that your advertising dollars are being well spent, however, it is necessary that some tracking mechanism is in effect.

Common modes of tracking include special telephone numbers reserved for special ads, coded response cards that indicate which ad is being responded to, and, as stated, simply asking those who call where they heard of your firm.

SHOULD YOU USE AN ADVERTISING AGENCY?

Small firms and sole practitioners may be able to rely on the assistance of newspaper and directory advertising sales personnel to assist them in the design and wording of simple ads, but an agency should be used if a video, radio, or television ad is to be produced to ensure that quality and a professional appearance or sound is obtained.

Agencies can also help you make informed decisions as to where you might place your ads most effectively and most efficiently, based on demographic studies and market research, as well as the experience to help you plan a mix of advertising to help you meet your goals. And they generally have the art, design, copywriting, and printing or production expertise to meet your needs.

WRITING YOUR OWN DIRECT-MAIL ADVERTISING COPY

Direct-mail advertising may be the most cost-effective way in which to reach your audience, or, if not done well, a waste of time and money.

There are some time-honored rules for successful direct-mail advertising. They include the following:

1. There must be a present need for the service you are marketing. For selling products, an advertiser may be able to create a need, but for legal services, the need must be preexisting.

2. Your offer to provide services must be reasonable and should indicate, within the guidelines of your state's rules for professional conduct, why it is that the potential client should choose to use your services rather than someone else's.

3. When you write the ad, write it to be read from the readers' standpoint, not your own. Show the reader how she or he will benefit from using your services, and write it in terms that the reader will not only understand, but be comfortable with. Advertising copywriter Victor Schwab recommends the use of his AAPPA formula for writing good copy:

A—Get *Attention.*

A—Show People an *Advantage.*

P —*Prove* It.

P —*Persuade* People to Grasp this Advantage.

A—Ask for *Action.*

Other prominent copywriters have suggested that effective copy will promise the benefit in the headline or first paragraph, much like a short story or magazine article has a hook that grabs the reader's attention early on and entices them to read on. *Advertising Age's* checklist for better direct-mail copy, first published in that magazine's March 25, 1968 issue, is still a valuable reference for copywriters. Among its most helpful hints are tips on using "you" throughout the piece, using a conversational tone, using 70–80 percent one-syllable words, avoiding beginning sentences with A, An, or The if at all possible, and using short paragraphs (no more than six lines) packed with action verbs. The paragraphs should be tied together with what has been called a "bucket brigade" of transitional devices, examples of which include terms such as "But that's not all," "Moreover," "But there is one more reason," and "So call us today."

4. The most important aspect of direct-mail advertising is to make sure that the list you use is one that offers the best prospects for the services you use. The best-crafted direct-mail letter, sent to an audience that will *never* have the need for the service you advertise, will be of absolutely no value to you. Good lists, rented from reputable list brokers, should also be culled frequently by the broker to make sure that bad addresses are kept to a minimum.

REFERENCES

There are many valuable reference works on creating effective advertising. The one I recommend most highly is the *Advertising Manager's Handbook,* published by Dartnell Corporation (800–621–5463). It costs $19.95 and provides in-depth, practical advice on all aspects of advertising in print, direct mail, and electronic media.

Other books I have found useful are *Profitable Advertising Techniques for Small Business,* by Harvey R. Cook (Reston) and *How To Be Your Own Advertising Agency,* by Bert Holtje (McGraw-Hill).

Chapter Eight

How to Start a Client Newsletter

ABOUT DESKTOP PUBLISHING

I got into desktop publishing six years ago when, believe it or not, desktop publishing was in its infancy. Now, the proliferation of self-publishing software programs means that nearly anyone with a computer can put together a newsletter.

That doesn't mean people will read it, and it certainly doesn't mean it will be any good. Anyone with a can of paint and a brush can paint a picture, too.

Desktop publishing software does not create publications, people do. Desktop publishing software's advantages are in saving a publisher's time and money. How?

You lay out a page on your monitor and in the blink of an eye you can change the layout, add copy, enlarge a picture, even change the name on the masthead. With paste-ups, that would take hours. The danger, of course, is that the novice desktop publisher never stops fooling around with the layout, it's so much fun to change it.

Desktop publishers wear more than one hat, too. Not all that long ago, type was set by typographers in type houses using either casting (hot lead), hand-set type from a job case, or photocomposition (cold type). Now, desktop publishers select the fonts and sizes from computer software lists that would boggle the mind of a linotype operator. The danger, here, is that with so many fonts to choose from the ultimate purpose of type, making the copy readable, sometimes gets lost. The beauty, of course, is that desktop publishers who know how to use type well can create pages that captivate their readers.

And, with desktop publishing and a good copier, the need for printing on a small run is eliminated; the desktop publisher is often designer, writer, editor, typesetter, and printer.

This chapter is designed to help beginning desktop publishers who would like to use their hard- and software, as well as their creativity, to start a marketing tool that is informative, attractive and well received by its readership.

WHY A NEWSLETTER?

We are not unlike cows in a way; we enjoy being with our herdmates. We like to be with people who share our ideas, our interests, our experiences. It reinforces our sense of self-worth, creates new professional contacts, gives us a chance to learn more about what we already like to do, and helps us to do it better.

Your clients will enjoy a newsletter that keeps them up-to-date on changes in the law that affect their business and personal lives, particularly if it gives them practical tips on how to be more profitable, pay less taxes, or prepare for their retirement.

Newsletters are an inexpensive way to be herdmates, even across vast distances. Wherever the mail goes (or now, even fax lines), the newsletter goes too, carrying business reports, recipes, political views, notions of how to tie the best trout fly, and what-have-you to an audience that is interested in the same things.

And creating and running a newsletter is a satisfying endeavor that brings you into contact with very interesting people, and one which sharpens the many skills needed to successfully launch and run one. A newsletter can also be a sound marketing tool for getting your name and the services you provide before a large number of people for a relatively small amount of money without the look or feel of direct mail.

A good newsletter contains news, and therefore has some utility to the recipient. You may even be able to turn a well-designed, well-thought-out newsletter into a profit center, or one at least in which paying subscribers offset some, if not all of the costs of production and mailing.

But it's not as easy as it looks, and there are lots of things to learn and consider before popping a ream in the mail. Remember that the newsletter's professionalism, utility, and readability will be representative of your ability in the client's eyes.

Tailor Newsletters to Your Clients' Needs

"There are a lot of good ideas, out there," an entrepreneur once told me, "but not all of them will work."

Not because the ideas aren't good. It might be because there isn't enough money to develop and market them, or the target audience is too small or ill-defined to attract customers, or there simply just isn't enough new news to justify the creation of a publication for a particular set of clients.

I like to paint pictures of choppy seas, for example. No boats. Just choppy seas and dark, foreboding skies. I like them. My wife says she likes them, too. But I doubt that I could ever launch a successful newsletter on "How to Paint Choppy Seas Without Boats." How would I ever find enough people interested in such an arcane hobby willing to pay enough to cover the costs of printing and mailing the piece?

Finding a niche in today's publishing market for any set of potential clients is a difficult task and requires research. Fortunately, most of that research has been done for you by companies called "list firms." They maintain and sell (for somewhere between $45 and $75 or more per thousand names) mailing lists of people and companies with a great variety of demographic criteria and shared interests or experiences in common.

These lists are rented or purchased by those firms from list brokers, who, in turn, either generate them by direct-mail requests for information or purchase them from others like magazine publishers or, the biggest list producers of all, the US Postal Service, the Internal Revenue Service, and telephone companies.

Knowing that you can purchase a great deal of the necessary information is half the battle, however. You must also know *what information to ask for.*

Let's Find a Niche

Let's pretend that what you want to do is start a newsletter for people who own their own businesses and need periodic advice on the law as it applies to small businesses. It's an area of the law in which you have a great deal of experience and you'd like to share information with others in the hope of attracting new clients.

Sounds like a good idea to you (and to me), so you decide to check it out.

First, Check the Market

Is it already saturated with publications like the one you're thinking about? The Index to Periodicals at your library is a good place to start. So are good bookstores, especially those with computers that permit you to search subject areas by key words like "small business," "sole proprietors," and so forth. And you can check other references, too, like *Writer's Market,* an annual publication of Writer's Digest Books that lists many book, magazine, and newsletter publishers who are looking for freelance writers.

You should also check the Yellow Pages of Washington, DC, New York, Chicago, Los Angeles, and other large cities where not-for-profit associations are generally headquartered. If enough people like to do something, chances are someone has formed an association for them and is in the business of publishing a periodical for its membership.

In checking the market, you are also gaining valuable information as to the potential lists you may want to buy. For example, if you find a magazine entitled *"Legal Issues For Small Businesses,"* you might want to purchase their mailing list directly or through a list firm. Of course, after reading an issue or two of *"Legal Issues For Small Businesses"* you may also decide that the information provided by that publication is just what you wanted to provide, and, even though only one magazine is on the market, your market is saturated, nonetheless. But, for our purposes, we will assume that it is not.

Also, you should check the market for book stores, and vendors of computer software programs and office supplies that cater to small businesses. Jot down the names of the publishing houses and firms that sell to your potential clients. Write to them and ask for information on their lists and whether they have any publications they send to the people who buy their products. Again, you are not only determining whether there is a niche large enough to accommodate your proposed newsletter, you are also defining your target audience.

And, in today's automated world, there are also the computer bill-boards like those on the interactive service *Prodigy.* You can place a note (free to members) asking others if they are interested in small business legal issues. You should also post electronic notes inquiring as to whether there are any such bulletin boards that are dedicated to small business topics. The annual fees for admittance to such bulletin boards are usually small, if there is a fee at all.

There are many sources to check and learn from. You might even call one or more of the list firms to see whether they have a list of small businesses and, if so, what demographic information is available about them—average ages of the owners, whether they have college degrees, how much they spend on legal fees—information that may be very important later, as we will see.

Analyze the Data

Assume that we've found out that there are two magazines that deal exclusively with small businesses, but they offer limited information on how legal issues, such as the Americans with Disabilities Act, will impact on them. The subscribers to those magazines seem like prime candidates to be recipients of your newsletter. You have also found that there is an association, The US National Association of Small Business People of America, that has more than 2,000 members. Again, a source of potential subscribers as well as, perhaps, contributors in some way to your newsletter.

Your note on the computer bulletin boards generated 25 responses. That's another 25 subscribers.

And you have discovered that companies who sell office supplies and computer software to small businesses have mailing lists that number more than 10,000, combined.

So, after one week of research, you know that the market *might* support a newsletter such as yours. Publishing is nothing more than problem solving within a new framework of possible solutions. The problem now is to find out how to cost-effectively determine whether the *potential* subscribers can be turned into *actual* subscribers who have the potential of becoming clients.

To Find Subscribers or Not

A few telephone calls later, you know that you can purchase mailing lists that are updated monthly of more than 10,000 people who *might* be interested in paying for a subscription to your as-yet unnamed newsletter. But you have also learned that you have at your disposal the names and addresses of more than 10,000 people who are small businesspeople. A newsletter addressed to them with reasonable advertising rates might be attractive to the companies and people who sell goods and services such people need. Reasonable advertising rates are rates that get an advertiser's message to its target audience cheaper than any other way.

If you decide to try to get subscribers, you have to set a price for your newsletter that covers all of your costs, is affordable and attractive, and perhaps provides a modest profit for your labors. You also have to make a commitment to fulfilling your promise to those subscribers. If you promise four issues a year for $4, you better have enough staying power to cover the costs of putting together four issues and mailing them, or the ability to refund their money if you can't.

And you have to sell the publication to them. Just because the potential pool of subscribers share common interests, it doesn't mean they'll buy your newsletter. It has to be sold to them. You have to show them why your publication offers them something they can't get anywhere else and why that something will make them more profitable in their business or provide them with more leisure time or some other benefit.

What makes your newsletter better than any other? What does it offer that none other offers? How does it make the subscribers' lives better? How you answer these questions will help to determine the name of your publication, its layout, and its content. In effect, these answers determine the newsletter's niche within a niche, what space on the coffee table it will occupy, and for how long.

Or No Subscribers at All

If you decide not to attract paying subscribers, you will have to fund your publication in another way, either out of your firms's marketing/advertising budget or through the sale of advertising space in it to companies and individuals seeking to market their goods and services to that same pool of people you have uncovered. Selling ads is a labor-intensive process that also means developing advertising press kits, finding the competition's prices and share of the market, and convincing advertisers with long, established relationships with other publications that they're better off dumping an effective vehicle for their message for one that is untried and, as yet, unpublished. It's called "selling air," and it's challenging, if not a nightmare.

Making the decision to be "driven" by ad sales alone affects the layout of the newsletter (you have to leave space for the ads), its frequency (you may find that instead of a September issue, the advertisers prefer a preholiday, October market in which to advertise), and its content as well (some advertisers want "advertorials"—articles that look like editorial writing but are really ads made to look and read like stories). Such stories should have the word "Advertisement" printed above and below them, if you permit them, which I would not).

I advise new publications to go for the subscribers or to cover the cost of production all by themselves for three reasons:

1. If your idea is good enough to attract subscribers, the advertisers will follow, someday. Selling advertising then will be a decision made not of necessity, but for the right business reasons.

2. Advertisers will be hard to convince to jump onto your bandwagon until you've proven yourself and your publication. You could go broke in the meantime, publishing a newsletter that thousands read for free.

3. If you get no subscribers, chances are your idea wasn't as good as you thought it was. Better to get out with the minimum number of scrapes and bruises.

GETTING SUBSCRIBERS, PART ONE

Remember those three questions we faced just a few paragraphs ago?

What makes your newsletter better than any of the others?

What does it offer that none other does?

How does it make subscribers' lives better?

It's time to answer them, because before you try to interest subscribers in your publication, that publication needs to be well defined and planned. In answering them, look to the competition and find out not only what they do but, more importantly, what they don't do.

Sometimes what they don't do will literally jump out at you. A small business magazine that doesn't have articles on "How the New Tax Law Affects Point of Purchase Advertising," "How to Obtain Free Liability Insurance," or "Close Corporation Accounting: Key Ways to Save Thousands" will give you plenty of ideas. Sometimes, the letters to the editor of those publications will provide insight into what their readerships may want to see more of.

Study the competition and imagine what articles, columns, advice, and how-to sections would be most interesting to you. If they interest you and you know something about small business, chances are your readers will find them interesting, too.

Which brings me to an important point: Every publication is different because, ultimately, it is the result of one person's vision. Never lose your focus or your vision. You can change it, but never lose it in an attempt to be like everything else on the market. Nobody buys copycat products. They want things that are fresh and interesting. Be different to be successful.

As you come up with ideas that are compatible with your initial vision of what your newsletter should be, yet different from those of other publications, jot them down and keep them in a notebook or on the hard drive of your computer. Add to them daily. The vast majority of ideas will never be used, but if you get one good idea out of 100, you're doing great.

After a while, you will see that your list of topic ideas is becoming more focused, narrower. You might find, for example, that the story lines seem to have a common thread, a specialized niche no one else has targeted. Suddenly, you feel a surge of excitement that says, Wow! I have hit my niche and it's something that excites me! It must be right!

Develop a More Focused Target Audience for Your Test Mailing

You need to further and continually redefine the scope of your newsletter as well as the target audience for your test mailing and future subscription sales efforts. That means knowing the market better than anyone else.

It doesn't make sense, for example, to send a subscription plea for a newsletter about native brown trout fly fishing to someone in Arizona. Arizona has no native brown trout. You should focus your efforts instead on those potential subscribers most likely to fly fish for native brown trout near where they live.

The lists you discovered earlier are usually, if not always, available on a ZIP code basis. Find out where the small business people are who are the most likely targets for this aspect of your marketing effort, get their ZIP codes, and select those who live closest to you. But, before you buy any lists, put up any coupon cards, or do anything else, it's time to settle on a basic cover design and give a name to the publication. After that's done, we'll come back to Getting Subscribers, Part Two.

THE ELEMENTS OF DESIGN

The purpose of the design of a newsletter, much the same as the design of a newspaper, magazine, or advertisement, should be to encourage people to read it, to get your message across. It's as simple as that. Any design or typographical elements that detract from the readability of the piece should be avoided, despite how beautiful or daring others may think they are. Your goal is to gain a dedicated following that will someday turn to you for legal advice, not to create a new art form.

The design of your newsletter should also add something to the understanding of the editorial. A picture is worth a thousand words is an old adage, but as print communications become more and more complex, the adage takes on new meaning. Ask anyone who has tried to connect a computer to all of its peripherals without a diagram.

Your newsletter's design should also be distinctly that of *your* newsletter; it should be such that when people see it again, they will recognize it. The placement of the headline and logo, the number and widths of the columns, the number of pages, and placement of columns and departments and mailing labels—all of the building blocks should be assembled in a predictable manner so as not to confuse your readers from issue to issue.

Even if you are dissatisfied with the initial design, *don't change it right away.* Your readers will develop a sense that since the design is not permanent, the publication might also be fleeting. Besides, the US Postal Service defines a periodical qualifying for second-class rates in part as one that "must . . . exhibit continuity from issue to issue. Continuity may be evidenced by serialization of articles or by successive issues carrying the same style, format, theme or subject matter."

The logo you select, if you use one, should be able to stand on its own, add to the understanding of the subject matter your newsletter covers, and be as instantly recognizable (after your readers get used to it) as the Pepsi logo without the word "Pepsi." I'll bet the image of the Pepsi logo just flashed through your mind as you read that. That is what you should strive for.

The color(s) of the paper stock you choose as well as the basis weight of the paper, its texture and coating, the type you spec for the various textual elements, the art/photography selected, how much "white" or "negative space" is used, whether you print in one, two, or four colors—each of these decisions will affect the readability and feel of the publication and should be considered when determining the feel you want the piece to have.

For example, our small business newsletter will be developed to appeal, our demographic information tells us, to men and women who have less than 20 employees, enjoy average annual profits of $500,000 on sales of $6 million, and are engaged in service (60 percent) or consumer product (40 percent) industries. Our demographic analyses tell us they have above-average incomes and are college-educated for the most part, and many have advanced degrees. They take their business seriously and are very conservative.

They do not want neon-colored paper. They do not want blaring headlines. They do not want avant-garde typefaces.

If there's to be excitement, it should come from the discovery of something they have yet to think of, something that improves performance on the bottom line. Or an article about how productivity can be augmented by using legal software products that reduce the time required to complete contracts.

Close your eyes. Think about these things for a minute and think "color."

No-nonsense white background, crisp blue headlines, sharp black copy come to mind.

Now close your eyes again and think "texture."

For me, a heavy, rough linen stock comes to mind, something sturdy and durable, a paper that says "quality" but not "expensive." (Paper stocks should conform to postal regulations and be sturdy enough to stand up to mailing.)

Now close your eyes again and think "type."

That's a tougher question for most people, simply because they are not as accustomed to thinking about typography as they are colors and textures. We think about colors and textures when we buy clothes, select wallpaper, or decide how to paint the kids' bedrooms. Typography rarely enters our minds, yet it affects our decisions as to what we read, how we read, and how we feel about what we read every day.

About Type

As an exercise in beginning to understand the basics of typography, go to a bookstore that has a healthy display of magazines. You will be able to pick out the ones that are designed to appeal to children, those designed for teens, and the ones designed for men and for women, simply by the typefaces used on their covers.

In order to discuss the reason you can make these determinations, you should have some understanding of the basics of type terminology.

The text type used in this book is called Times Roman. I selected Times Roman for three reasons:

I like it. That may seem flip, but if I'm going to be running a newsletter and setting type for it, issue after issue, I want to like not only what I'm doing, but how I'm doing it as well.

It's a serif type. A *serif* is the stroke that projects from the top or bottom of the main stroke of the letter. (See Figure 1.) Serif typefaces are easier

FIGURE 1

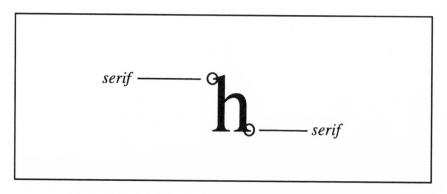

to read than sans serif type. The little strokes seem to help the letters and words flow together. In Figure 2, the same paragraphs are set in two separate types, the top one in Times Roman and the bottom in Helvetica, a sans serif font. See which one seems easier for you to read.

Times Roman is a commonly used, comfortable type that people are used to reading. No surprises to alarm or otherwise upset the reader looking for ways to relax. It is also a dignified type face, without curly-Qs or flourishes.

The size of the type used in this text is 11 point, a very commonly used size, and the leading, or vertical distance between the rows of type, is 2 points, making the type more readable than if there were no leading whatsoever. Eleven point type set with 2 point leading is referred to by designers and typographers as "11/13" (11 over 13). If there were no leading and 10 point type were used, we would call it "10 over 10," and 10 point type set with 3 point leading is referred to as "10 over 13."

In Figure 3, you will see the differences in readability caused by different degrees of leading in the type. Some leading improves readability; too much makes reading difficult.

For a more modern newsletter that deals with high-tech gadgetry, I might be more inclined to use a sans serif typeface, one that says "New!" Note that whenever sans serif type is used, leading must also be used to improve the horizontal flow.

Another exercise: This one you can do in your kitchen. Get out boxes of cereal, soup cans, spice bottles, and other packaged goods. Are their

FIGURE 2

This paragraph is set in Times Roman, a serif font that many find easy to read. The serifs permit the type to flow easily, unlike the sans serif type in the following paragraph. Sans serif fonts are often used in headlines and in logos to give the impression that what is being discussed is modern, new, and up-to-date. If you were to browse through a bookstore and look at the titles of magazines, you may notice that periodicals designed to appeal to young audiences have logos and cover blurbs set in a sans serif font. Conversely, those designed to appeal to older audiences are usually set in a serif font. That may, of course, change, as the younger readers age.

This paragraph, by way of contrast, is set in Helvetica, a sans serif font, that many find more difficult to read in text. It is used more frequently for headlines, subheads, captions, blurbs, direct mail attention-grabbers, and so forth. These are only two examples of type styles. The varieties of type are bound only by the imagination. One particularly impressive font I once saw was the name of a city, seemingly carved out of granite, with the tops of the letters crumbling. The type not only gave the title of the story that followed, but set the mood, the tone, and the story line for the piece. Both paragraphs are set in the same size of type, 10 point.

FIGURE 3

10/10

This paragraph is set in Times Roman, a serif font that many find easy to read. The serifs permit the type to flow easily, unlike the sans serif type in the following paragraph. Sans serif fonts are often used in headlines and in logos to give the impression that what is being discussed is modern, new, and up-to-date. If you were to browse through a bookstore and look at the titles of magazines, you may notice that periodicals designed to appeal to young audiences have logos and cover blurbs set in a sans serif font. Conversely, those designed to appeal to older audiences are usually set in a serif font. That may, of course, change, as the younger readers age.

10/12

This paragraph is set in Times Roman, a serif font that many find easy to read. The serifs permit the type to flow easily, unlike the sans serif type in the following paragraph. Sans serif fonts are often used in headlines and in logos to give the impression that what is being discussed is modern, new, and up-to-date. If you were to browse through a bookstore and look at the titles of magazines, you may notice that periodicals designed to appeal to young audiences have logos and cover blurbs set in a sans serif font. Conversely, those designed to appeal to older audiences are usually set in a serif font. That may, of course, change, as the younger readers age.

typefaces saying "New?" or "So tried and true, your mother relied upon them?" Heinz Worcester Sauce's label is in a heavy serif face. It says, "Solid, Unchanged, Always Good, Always Will Be." Bisquick, by comparison, has retained the colors of its packaging, so as to maintain identifiability on the grocery store shelves, but its logo is now in a sans serif. It is trying to say, "You know us from our colors, but we're just as modern as anything else around us."

If you are unsure as to what text type to use, choose first the typefaces that you feel most comfortable with. If you are like your readers, chances are they will like your choice, too. Don't choose anything flashy unless "flashy" is what you want to say. And remember the age of your readers. You will be competing with thousands of other images calculated to get their attention every day. What appeals to an adolescent girl will not appeal to a 50-year-old man, and vice versa.

As far as type for headlines and subheads (see Figure 4), you can sometimes get away with a sans serif type, even when the text is serif, in a magazine where there are many pages to play with and articles appealing to different sets of people are laid out differently. For a four- or eight-page newsletter, however, stick to one or the other, using different sizes, boldfacing, and italics to gain variety.

About Logos

We already know that the logo should convey something about the content and spirit of the publication, be designed to be easily identifiable, and be unique. With those constraints in order, let's design a logo and a title for our small business newsletter.

FIGURE 4

What's the newsletter about? Small business, law, regulations, safety, innovation, saving money, quality, productivity enhancements, and so forth.

Somewhere in that laundry list lurk both logo and a title. If you select the title first, it helps you design the logo. If you select the logo first, it helps you create the title.

In this case, let's opt for the logo first. The images that come to my mind first are a simple headline and a graph that reinforces the idea of business.

Titles

Entitling a new publication is a serious undertaking. You can change layout periodically, you can change column width and departments, but if you change the title you confuse your readership and also create a morass of paperwork with the postal service, including applying for a new second-class permit (if you have subscribers), and with the Library of Congress, from which you obtain your ISSN.

First, the title should not be currently used or registered as a trademark or service mark by anyone else. This can be determined by contacting the Secretaries of State of the states to which you plan to mail.

Second, it should be distinctive, easy to read, and pack a lot of information into very few words. *Ladies Home Journal* is for *ladies,* who can afford to stay at *home* and decorate it to their liking, and the word *journal* denotes that they are well educated.

Third, it should be sufficiently specific to set your newsletter apart from others.

Given the range of activities for which our newsletter is being developed and the logo we have selected, the following titles seem appropriate, although you are encouraged to come up with others as an exercise:

Small Business Law.

The Small Business Legal Reporter.

Legal Trends for Small Business.

Business Law.

Of the above, I like "Small Business Law" the best, although to get the point of the newsletter across, I would add a subhead (an additional line of title in smaller type below it), as in Figure 5.

Seems to say it all without ambiguity, and the logo reinforces the title.

FIGURE 5

Page Design

Many desktop publishing software programs come with newsletter formats already designed, ready for you to plug in the words and pictures. That's fine for some people, but I think a newsletter publisher ought to at least know the basics of page design and layout. There will be times you want to stray from a rigid grid and have fun. Besides, only you know how your newsletter is best designed to get the information across.

Here, we will examine some of the many possibilities for designing a four-page newsletter.

The Front Page

The front page is the most important page because it must attract the reader's interest long enough for him or her to pick it up and begin to read. Then it has to have enough to say to keep the reader interested. Powerful, grabbing headlines, pleasing design, pictures or drawings that are compelling, and leads that pull the reader into the story—these are the components of a great front page.

Figure 6 details a basic front page of a newsletter designed using Aldus Pagemaker software. The solid lines are "rules," used to separate text from other elements, to define the margins, and to lead the reader's eyes.

You will notice that "holes" (black areas) have been left for art and for "pull quotes" from the articles (teasers that grab the reader's attention and then jump to another page).

Below the title block is a line for type that addresses the price and volume and issue numbers of the publication as well as the date of the particular issue. This information is useful in convincing the postal

FIGURE 6

service that there is continuity of publication and also helps readers who wish to keep track of the issues. For that same reason, issues should be marked to be die cut for a three-ring binder.

Interior Pages: the Spread

Pages two and three of this newsletter can be used as a "spread," sometimes called a "double truck," or as single pages, depending upon the desires of the editor. In a four-page newsletter, space is at a premium, and the use of a spread to print a story should be reserved for truly exceptional stories. Otherwise, use the pages as singles.

Remember, however, that when you design these pages, they will both be visible to the reader at the same time, so the formats must be compatible with each other and viewed, optically and from the standpoint of the designer, as a spread. Therefore, they must balance to the eye.

Figure 7 is an example of how the interior, facing pages of a newsletter may be designed using both pages for a single textual message and making optimum use of good art. Note the column width. For readability, a column should never be more than two and one-half alphabets (65 characters) in length.

If you are interested in attracting advertisers, the lower half of page three is a good place to leave open for space sales. Advertisers will be pleased to be in the spread, and it simplifies the use of page four (the back cover) for carryover text, the mailing label "key," and information required by the postal service.

Figure 8 details the use of the back cover and explains what information is required to be printed on periodicals such as newsletters.

Interactive Devices

Throughout this book there are self-evaluation quizzes that reinforce major chapter points and help to focus the reader's attention on self-improvement for quality's sake. Hopefully, you have already taken pencil in hand and completed a few.

They also have another function in a newsletter. They involve the reader more deeply in the publication and that generates a sense of partnership. Properly designed, the quizzes are positive in tone and seek to increase the taker's self-esteem as well as his or her knowledge.

Such interactive devices may be incorporated in a client newsletter, as can stock cartoons that illustrate important issues in a humorous way. Getting the potential clients to enjoy the newsletter is an important step in getting them to pick up the phone and call for advice.

FIGURE 7

small business LAW

How to plan with your lawyer

Production Costs
Unit Price
Profits

200
195
190
165
160
155
150

1990 1991 1992

of Dollars

"The first step is to hire the right lawyer"

2

Planning for the future of your company may be one of the most important, and fruitful, decisions you can make. But it takes more than setting an appointment to discuss what the changes in the law may hold in store for your company.

Ideally, your lawyer should be a partner in your business, a valued member of your staff who is not a stranger to planning sessions. He or she should know your business, know your goals, and know the people who work with you to achieve them.

That kind of relationship takes time to develop. It starts with the decision on your part to find a lawyer who is right for your firm. First of all, don't wait until you need a lawyer. Hire one with the same amount of effort as you would your vice president or administrative assistant. And make sure that the commitment he or she is willing to make to representing your firm is what you want it to be.

How can you measure that level of commitment? There are four, proven ways that you can use to tell. First,

continued on page 4

3

FIGURE 8

Recent Federal Decisions Of Note:

cont'd from page 1
OSHA Changes

small business LAW
PO Box 123
Anytown, USA

Postage
Paid
Permit
No.1

WRITING THE NEWSLETTER

While you should determine what your newsletter should cover, it can be written and laid out by a professional writer for less than your time is worth. An excellent newsletter writer can research and write a four-page publication for less than $500 an issue; laying out the first one may cost several hundred dollars because it must be formatted, but subsequent issues should not cost more than $100 additional.

Using a professional will ensure that your message gets across in a way that is designed to appeal to your target audience. A good newsletter writer will be able to alter his or her style and language to appeal to audiences with different levels of education, experience, and reading ability, as well as different business, professional, or personal orientations.

There are many good freelance public relations writers available. Make sure you find one who has done newsletters before and can show you samples of his or her work.

After several issues, you may discover that they are able to generate interesting story lines for you. But you should always retain the final authority over what is printed and the way in which it is written. And, it should go without saying that you should read and approve all the copy. It would be embarrassing indeed to have a potential client call to discuss the fine points of an article in your newsletter that you had neglected to read.

GETTING SUBSCRIBERS, PART TWO

Leave room in your newsletter for a coupon that potential subscribers can clip and send to you to make sure they get on the mailing list. Or, print a phone number they can call (toll free would be nice) to subscribe. Do this whether you plan to charge a subscription price or not. It provides you with a means to track the success of your newsletter.

Also, provide a "letters to the editor" column for people to write in with questions or comments. The comments you receive will help you shape the newsletter to respond to the needs of the marketplace, rather than your perception of what those needs are.

Establish a realistic goal for your newsletter, a 3 percent subscription rate after four issues, for example, and a certain number of new clients, depending upon the number of newsletters you mail.

After the first two issues have been mailed, do a follow-up mailing with a survey that can be completed quickly by the recipient and returned in a business reply envelope. If you ask the recipient to pay postage, your response rate will be low.

Ask the recipients what they like and what they don't like, how the newsletter could be changed to help them in their business, and what kinds of articles they would like to read about in future issues.

By giving them the power to change the publication, you are again inviting them to become your partner and demonstrating that you put their interests, their needs, their desires first.

Then follow up on their suggestions and give them what they want. Remember, quality is in the eyes of the client.

A Newsletter Grows and Changes

Allow your newsletter the freedom to grow, change, and adapt to the demands of its readership. Keep it free of personal ego. Don't put your picture in it, or that of your fellow attorneys. Put your subscribers' pictures in it, if they send them to you. Make it their newsletter to the extent that you can without hurting its mission.

The more your readers want to be included, however, the more your newsletter is doing its job as a marketing tool for your practice.

A Simpler Way

There is, of course, a simpler way to obtain a newsletter to send to clients, particularly if your client base is composed primarily of individuals. You can buy the "canned" newsletters and have your name, address, and telephone number printed on them. All you have to do then is send them out.

The American Bar Association's Division for Public Education publishes a series of quarterly newsletters entitled "Your Law" for sale to practitioners. Each four-page issue is printed in two colors with attractive graphics. An example is shown in Appendix A.

The ABA's "Your Law" series is, however, necessarily generic in content; the issues are prepared for distribution throughout the United States, so the topics and discussions are general in nature, and not state-specific. Examples of subjects covered in recent issues include "Get it in Writing" (contract law); "Child's Best Interests" (custody); "Bankruptcy;" and "Family Matters in Estate Planning."

A small firm or sole practitioner may find these newsletters quite valuable for staying in contact with clients. For more information about "Your Law," contact the ABA at 541 N. Fairbanks Court, Chicago, IL 60611–3314, or call 312–988–5729. At this writing, the costs of obtaining a sufficient quantity of copies to mail one issue to 100 clients each quarter, imprinted with a firm's name, address, and telephone number, is $175.

Other Ways

If the canned newsletters are too generic for your practice, or offer too little in the way of specific guidance for your clients' needs, the ABA will also license the right to use excerpts from its book, *You and the Law,* a mammoth tome that contains virtually every subject the general practitioner will encounter. Unlike the "Your Law" newsletters, it contains state-specific matters. It is updated infrequently, however, so care must be exercised to ensure that the information provided is current.

Of course, using excerpts from *You and the Law* means that you will have to create a newsletter format as discussed earlier in this chapter.

Chapter Nine

Training Your Staff

Hire a consultant to help you get your marketing and quality programs started, but once the consultant leaves, it's your job to make sure the training is implemented.

To be effective, the training should ideally be firmwide, although experts caution against spending precious training dollars on reluctant participants. What sort of training each staff member receives will, to some degree, depend upon their amount of client contact and their particular duties.

Secretarial personnel, for example, might be trained to better use the telephone, to ensure that all documents are produced error-free, to treat clients as though they were the most important people in the world (they are) without fawning over them, to make sure that files are current and easily accessible, to use tickler files to avoid last-minute rushes or missed deadlines, and to maintain quality as a goal in all matters.

Attorneys, on the other hand, in addition to improving client relations, might be trained to cross-sell the services of other lawyers in the firm, to become better salespersons of their own skills, and to improve their writing and oral presentation skills for courtroom as well as other, less formal, occasions. They should also be trained in personnel matters: how to interview prospective employees; to recognize the inherent worth and usefulness of staff, regardless of position; to be more sensitive to the personal and professional needs of others; in short, to be better people-managers.

But all personnel should be trained in how to set and attain goals, how to motivate others for the greatest possible productivity, how to function as a team member as well as a team leader when the situation calls for it, and how to continually seek self-improvement and develop skills that further the marketing efforts of the firm and increase the quality of the services it renders its clients.

HIRE MARKETERS

The best, and cheapest, way to get personnel who will best market your firm's services is to hire with marketing in mind. It won't relieve you of the responsibility for instituting training programs to keep the edge sharp, but it will give you an advantage. And, they will teach others to market by example.

When you interview for support staff, or for associates as well, look for indicators that the individual being considered has the aptitude to sell as well as the technical competence to do the job.

What jobs have they held in the past? Did they seek out positions that had an emphasis on customer/client contact? Do they have any experience in direct sales? Did they take any courses in marketing or advertising that could benefit your firm tangentially? If you are looking to hire an attorney, don't overlook successful sole practitioners who may be interested in expanding the variety of services they can offer. Despite the reluctance of large firms to hire such people, they are usually adept at marketing themselves. Otherwise, they would not be successful.

Do they have an entrepreneurial spirit? People who have attempted to build their own business have an understanding of what it takes to keep a business running. They already know how important the customer or client is. People with an entrepreneurial bent also are not afraid to take risks and are comfortable trusting their instincts. Such people can be the source of creative solutions, if allowed the latitude to express themselves.

How do they sell themselves? When you finish the interview, just how impressed are you—not just with credentials, but with the person?

Once, while a sole practitioner, I was interviewing for a secretary, a very important position in a two-person office. I advertised the position and asked interested candidates to be at my office at 9 AM one Monday morning. I got there at 8 AM, and the crowd was already forming.

The applicants, all women, had a wide range of experiences, from certification as a paralegal in several cases, to years of experience working for other lawyers. I was already beginning to lose track of who was who when a young woman named Marsha Fedor entered my office.

Her resume was not impressive, to say the least. She was a high school graduate whose typing skills were fine, but her experience consisted primarily in working in a beer distributorship as secretary, accountant, bill payer, order clerk, and all-round gofer.

When I told her that I didn't see the experience I was looking for, she leaned forward and offered to work for me for free for two weeks, to show me that she could do the job better than anyone else. She wasn't pulling my leg. She really believed she could do it. I got the feeling that here was a young lady who had never failed at anything she had set her sights on. What an impression to give a prospective employer!

I hired her, of course. She stayed with me until I decided not to actively practice. She was the best secretary I ever had, and the best I will ever hope to have. She knew how to handle everything and everybody. She taught herself the job. I would scratch out interrogatories and leave them in her in-box. They would be properly filed and served within hours.

Clients, clerks at the courthouse, opposing counsel, everybody that came in contact with Marsha commented to me about what a fine secretary she was.

How she sold herself to me made me sure that she would sell herself, and my practice, to everyone she met, and I was right.

What do they offer you? Are the people you interview merely looking for a job or are they selling you a service? Some people expect a job, others want an opportunity to show what they can do. You know which one to hire. Do they answer your questions politely or do they go the extra step and tell you how they can make a difference if they're hired? Are they self-confident? Can they handle the curve ball as well as the pitch that's right over the plate?

In the interview, give them a real life problem in their area of expertise, something that has already happened at your firm and involved a problem with a client's case. Ask them how they would have solved it. How they respond will tell you how they might perform on the job. Assess their answers on the following bases:

Was their response creative? Did it reveal that they have the ability to seek innovative ways to reach a solution?

Did they ask for more information? Rather than go off half-cocked, the employee you're seeking is one that will have a firm grasp of the situation before jumping in blindly.

Did they consider the client in their answer? You want to hire people who will always have the client's interest and the firm's image at heart.

Did they consider the firm in their answer? The people you hire must be team players in the new sense of the word. They must consider what is best for the organization as a whole, and not just themselves. See if their answer reveals a desire to come out on top individually or whether they instinctively consider the feelings of other people on staff, including your own.

Look for the rainmaker. Later in this chapter, the traits of a successful "rainmaker," as developed by Business Development, Inc., are listed. Whenever you interview candidates for a new position at your firm, it's a good idea to keep this list near your desk. See how the candidates match up to the personality traits and work habits in that listing.

Fire them if they don't work out. A small law firm is no place to hide an antisocial personality or an individual who cannot, or will not, pull more than his or her own weight consistently. Chances are, the others on staff are just as anxious to see such people leave as you are, but the reasons for the discharge should be made known to all, if only to shut down the rumor mill.

SALESMANSHIP

Most of this book is about salesmanship. But the word "salesman" conjures up a Willy Loman kind of figure, more shoeshine than substance, relying upon a smile and fast talk to close a deal. You see that approach to salesmanship in the law, too, but it isn't effective at very many client levels. It seems too off-the-cuff, too unplanned to satisfy the needs of a sophisticated audience.

In a very real sense, salesmanship and planning are related. You can't determine the potential client's needs until you research the client or his business. You can't meet those needs until you research the law and determine the course of action that is not only best for the client, but most cost-effective, yet permits you to earn a living at the same time. You have to convince the prospective client that you are the logical choice for his legal service needs. And you can't implement the plan until you acquire the skills and materials to get the job done right.

Lord Thomson of Fleet, a Canadian newspaperman, once said that "The difference between rape and ecstasy is salesmanship." Though the example may be regarded as crude today, it has the seed of truth in it. Salesmanship is the art of getting others to buy what you want them to buy, even though they may not want to buy it, and then making them glad they did.

Successful salesmanship, also like successful leadership, has as its foundation mutual respect and trust. The potential client must trust in your ability to do what it is you claim you can do. Salesmanship, in the final analysis, is building that trust, and being unfailingly true to it.

BUILDING THE TRUST

Consistency of excellence in all matters.   That is the way to build trust. In the briefs you prepare and the way you dress, each act, insignificant as it may seem to you, may have significance in the eye of a client. Very early in my military career, before I was commissioned, I was standing inspection—rifle, boots, footlocker, clothes—by my cot in an old, wooden barracks building with the rest of my platoon. The prize was a weekend pass. Until the sergeant reached me, no one had passed the rifle inspection; he was able to find some grease, some grit, somewhere, if only in the magazine. My rifle was, however, spotless. I had boiled every metal part, including the magazine, in an immersion heater. I thought I had the pass in my pocket.

But I spent the weekend on post. Though you could shave in the reflection of the toes of my boots, the heels were scuffed. I'll never forget what the sergeant said: "The people in back of you have eyes, too!" It wasn't enough that I looked good enough for myself, I had to think of how others would see me as well.

Never give an offhand opinion.   Call it shooting from the hip, but no one likes the person who does it and gets caught. In the future, his or her advice will be taken with a grain of salt, if it's taken at all. In the same vein, support personnel should never say to clients, or prospective clients, "I think . . ." If they don't know the answer, they should say so, promise to find out, and guarantee an answer by a certain time and date. Then they should honor that guarantee.

Never offer a solution before you are fully aware of the problem or until you have had the opportunity to weigh its consequences.   If you do, the client may become enamored with it and demand that you follow up on it, even after you have discovered reasons why that solution may not be in his or her best interests. Besides, it's very difficult to go back to a client after you have made a recommendation and retract it. It will shake the client's confidence in you.

Let the client help lead you to the solution that is best for him or her. When trying to grasp the situation, couch suggestions in the form of questions such as, "If we were to approach the problem from this viewpoint, what problems, if any, would you anticipate from the shop steward?" Or, "What do you think your spouse would say if we were to offer $1,200 a month in alimony for a fixed term, say three years?" Very often, clients will have a feel for what will or won't work in a situation with which they are intimately familiar.

Never bluff.   Once found out, you will never be trusted again.

If you make a mistake, admit it.   As soon as possible, but not before you have researched ways to mitigate its damage, admit your mistake, unless greater harm will befall your client by waiting. It is far easier to forgive the person who can remedy the wrong than the person who merely brings bad news.

If you win a victory, don't revel in it.   Act as though a successful outcome was never in doubt. And, if you lose, don't blame anyone. Don't blame the judge, don't blame the witnesses, don't blame the weather. Suggest a meeting with your client in several days to discuss what steps can be taken to minimize the loss, appeal the decision, assess the damage, or put the matter to rest. That will give you time to regroup and look at the situation from a more detached standpoint.

Keep everything, including yourself, in perspective.   The noted American diplomat W. H. Page once said to Woodrow Wilson that "I once heard you say that it took you twenty years to recover from your legal training from the habit of mind that is bent on making out a case rather than on seeing the large facts of a case in their proportion." Don't be so much the lawyer that you fail to see the client's interests as compelling.

Always keep in mind the human cost of your actions.   If a particular course of action may have long-term effects that would be unacceptable to your client, advise him or her of those effects. A relative of mine once declared bankruptcy with the assurance from his lawyer that there would be no stigma attached to it. He was, as you probably are well aware, terribly wrong.

Never accept a matter you are not competent to handle. Unless you first ask other counsel to assist you, don't commit.

KEEPING THE TRUST

Someone once said that smiles don't keep customers, systems do. In order to keep your clients' trust, you must create systems to ensure that expected, positive behavior and results will recur. And those systems must be checked periodically to keep them fine-tuned.

Where can your office improve? What steps must be taken to improve? How can those steps be monitored? What procedure can be developed to make sure that the improvement becomes habit?

Those are the questions you need to ask your team when you begin to develop systems to make quality service more than buzz words.

If Susan the paralegal isn't getting the draft deposition digests to Steve the secretary in enough time to have them ready for your use, sit down with Susan and Steve and ask them what they can do to help alleviate the problem. Let them work out the system—*let them get an ownership interest in it*—and then monitor its effectiveness.

Encourage, at firmwide team meetings, everyone to bring up not just current problem areas, but areas in which they feel a problem might arise in the future, whether it has to do with client relations, billings, the quality of the work that leaves the office, staff morale, anything that should be improved to make your office more productive. Then establish the systems to correct those problems.

There is no checklist of areas in which systems should be created simply because they should be created in every area of your practice. Installing a word processing program with a spell-check feature will eliminate spelling errors only when it is used, and it will not correct grammatical errors. Only another system will do that. Having a tickler card system to remind you of when pleadings are due will only be as effective as the person referring to it. The first time the human element fails, develop a system to make sure it never happens again.

You may not achieve perfection, but you will be constantly striving for it.

CROSS-SELLING

If your firm has more than two lawyers, chances are it is involved in more than one area of practice and will, therefore, have more than one set of clients. Lawyer A's plaintiff client base will not be the same as Lawyer B's client base of people who need wills, trusts, and tax advice. In many such firms, the twain never meet.

But they should. A plaintiff who receives a settlement or verdict will experience a change that may well call for the services of Lawyer B to help him plan for his retirement and the future of his wife and children after he is gone. Conversely, Lawyer B's client, who is recovering from back surgery gone awry, may well benefit from a consultation with Lawyer A if there is a suspicion of malpractice on the surgeon's part.

Lawyers who fail to cross-sell their firm's services are missing an opportunity to increase not only their billings, but the quality of the legal services they provide their clients. *No client should ever have to seek another lawyer outside your firm if your firm can provide that service or associate with other counsel to provide it.*

In small firms, new clients, and old clients with new problems, should be the subject of discussion at regular meetings. Each lawyer should consider how his or her services might be used by the client.

Then the attorney with the established relationship should broach the subject with the client. "I talked this matter over with my partner, John Smith. He tells me that there's an interesting tax angle that you should be aware of. It could save you some money—more than the work involved would cost. Should I ask him to call you to set up an appointment?"

How could any client say no to a proposition that will save him or her money? It's a risk-free offer.

MARKETING TRAINING

Not everybody is a born salesperson, but everyone can improve their sales ability.

There are a number of firms that train attorneys to sell. Among them is Business Development, Inc., of Detroit, MI, a full-service resource for law firms that wish to increase their client base and improve profitability.

According to Julie Savarino, one of the firm's principals who is a lawyer and marketing professional, the largest problem with lawyers as salespeople is "They focus on themselves rather than their clients and their clients' needs. There is an overwhelming tendency among most professionals—lawyers, accountants, medical doctors—to have a similar tendency of focusing on their practice and not necessarily their clients."

To overcome that tendency, Julie educates them. "I teach them to put themselves in the client's shoes. It's a fallacy that clients care only about the results. Marketing studies show clients care very much about how they are treated. Having a well-developed set of client service skills is required to attract as well as to retain clients."

Her firm uses a variety of techniques to accomplish the training, but discovering what the performance objective is, and where the performance gaps are, is the first objective. The gaps, or areas of deficiency, may be in marketing knowledge, relationship management skills, how to target a market, how to cross-sell services, how to manage a seminar, how to write winning proposals, and how to build referral systems, among others.

"Then we determine the receptivity of the firm's attorneys to marketing," she says. "The people in the firm who are most receptive are the ones who should receive the training." Often, the nonprofessional employees should receive training too, because, as Julie recognizes, "They often have more client contact than the attorneys do."

Then, Julie encourages the firm to conduct a cost-benefit analysis to determine whether the training will accomplish the firm's goals. It also aids in determining which training options the firm can afford.

The rainmaker. Julie's work in the area of law firm marketing has led her to develop a list of the traits of the ideal "rainmaker," most of which can be taught through effective training.

Rainmaker Traits:

Motivated.

Enthusiastic.

Prompt.

Probing.

Assertive.

Dedicated to Follow-Up.

Honest.

Knows the Competition.

Knows the Firm.

Problem Solver.

Prepared.

Communicator.

Positive Attitude.

Patience.

Good Memory.

Likes People.

Creative.

Flexible.

Concerned.

DO YOU NEED MARKETING/SALES TRAINING?

To see if your firm's confidence in its ability to attract and retain clients
has led to complacency, Julie suggests that each lawyer in the firm take
the following quiz.

	Yes	No

1. Do you feel you've reached a level where sales training is not necessary?

2. Are you tempted to skip business development meetings or training sessions, thinking they are beneath you?

3. Do you brush off advice from colleagues because you feel you don't need their help?

4. Are you impatient with questions or suggestions regarding business development from others?

5. Do you pay little attention to marketing and business development aids
(such as training sessions, books, articles) because you think they have nothing new to tell you?

6. Do you record your business development efforts?

7. Are you hesitant to support the objectives of your firms such as target markets, new business from existing clients, etc.?

8. Do you feel you should be exempt from firm directives?

9. Does the amount of new business you generate stay about the same each
year?

10. Do you set annual business development goals?

If you answered yes to any questions other than 6 and 10, "Call Julie"
should take on a new meaning at your firm before you start digging for
new clients.

Rewards for top performers. For a very few people, performance is its own reward. Most others would like something tangible. For the rainmakers, it might be a percentage share in the work they bring in, early consideration for partnership, or a cash bonus predicated on the revenue they generate. Most corporations recognize that the best salesmen deserve rewards as an incentive to keep them producing as well as a disincentive for their leaving and taking their accounts with them.

But how many firms offer something to the best secretary of the month, the paralegal who found the one case on point that turned a losing proposition into one that could be dealt with, or the associate whose first argument was successful?

People want to know that their contributions are valued. They also want to be able to show their significant others that what they do from nine to five is respected and appreciated.

For them, a mention in the firm newsletter, if the firm is large enough to have one, or a gift certificate for two at a favorite restaurant will be incentive enough.

It is not the size of the reward for most people. It is the fact of the reward that motivates them.

And the peers of the achievers will want to excel too, to prove that they are equal to the task.

Any training program can afford some recognition for each of the people who contribute to the success of the firm.

The keys to successful training. The keys to successful training are providing information—the tools to do the job—and the motivation to get the job done right. What motivates one person to do a particular job may be vastly different from what would motivate another. One individual may wish to succeed in order to get material rewards, another to obtain the approval of someone in authority.

Similarly, the information, the training that should be given to each individual may vary according to the needs of the individual or, as Julie Savarino says, the "performance gaps" that dictate the need for training.

It is the responsibility of the leader in your firm to find out what those performance gaps are, either alone or with the help of a professional, and also to discover what will motivate each individual to enable him or her to become the most productive and sales-oriented member of your team possible.

Chapter Ten

Putting It All Together

Now that you have an understanding of the tools at your disposal for creating a marketing plan that is unique to your situation and specially designed to meet the goals you want to set for your practice, it's time to decide which tools to use, and how.

It is not necessary that all of the tools, community relations, public relations, electronic media advertising, direct mail, print ads, and the others, are used. Some may make sense in a particular context, others may not. But client-focused programs, the continual training of personnel, and seeking personal improvement, while leading those on your staff to seek the same, must be part of your plan.

It is that search for quality, as defined by your clients, that will make your marketing plan succeed, not the power of an ad's persuasive copy or the fact that you picked up the tab for an expensive client appreciation day dinner.

CREATING YOUR PLAN

In Chapter Two there is a blank, sample marketing plan. It's time to refer to that plan and fill in the blanks. Follow the steps below.

The examples stated are for a firm or sole practitioner that wishes to expand its practice to include the representation of individuals with claims of medical malpractice and are intended to be illustrative only.

Where to Begin

Begin with the formulation of your firm's mission statement, if you do not already have one. Refer to the discussion in Chapter Two, but remember, it should be created as a result of the collaborative efforts of each person in your firm, if each person is expected to feel as though they have an ownership interest in the firm and its future.

The mission statement, or value statement as it is sometimes called, should mirror the core of what your firm seeks to provide, not be a blueprint for the day-to-day operations. And it should be simple enough to be remembered by all. Domino's Pizza's mission statement, for example, says it all quite succinctly: "To deliver a hot, quality pizza in 30 minutes or less at a fair price and a reasonable profit."

In creating the mission statement, however, the most important rule is to make sure that it is one that you and everyone else in the firm can live with and apply every day. If the statement is too vague, too long, or couched in language that is difficult to understand, no one will remember it. If they can't remember it, it won't be there to guide them.

No one can write your mission statement for you; it must come from an understanding of what you are now and what you hope to be in the future.

Example: To provide our clients with the highest quality legal services possible, with an emphasis on medico-legal representation, regardless of the effort required, focusing on the needs and desires of the individual client, as he or she expresses them.

Setting the Overall Goal

Set the overall goal of your marketing plan. Make sure that it is couched in terms that are concrete and that it has a definite date for attainment.

Example: To offer, beginning March 1, 1996, comprehensive medico-legal representation to plaintiff clients that exceeds the quality of that offered by any other firm in the county.

Set your goal high enough to make you and the rest of the people in your firm stretch to meet it, but not so high that it appears unattainable. Nothing is more frustrating than being given an impossible task, but there are few things in life more rewarding than being given a difficult challenge, and meeting it successfully.

If your team balks at having goals set (and many do), start with simple goals and build upon them. As they succeed at small goals, your team will increase their ability and desire to tackle larger, more complex goals.

Think about an athletic team. They begin training by working on individual conditioning long before they attempt to bring their skills together as a group. They build upon their knowledge step by step, and that process builds trust in each other, and confidence in their shared ability to win.

Additional Skills Needed

What skills will be needed to reach this goal? Do you have those skills? Can you learn them in time to meet the deadline? Can you afford to hire personnel who already have those skills? Can you become an expert at delivering the proposed services? These are the next questions that have to be addressed.

Whatever the necessary skills are, now is the time to set goals to acquire them in time for you to meet the overall goal. If there are costs associated with obtaining those new skills, whether tuition, salaries and benefits for new employees or associates, or other expenditures, make sure that the increased revenues that can be reasonably expected from meeting the overall goal will justify the costs.

If you do not have the necessary skills and cannot acquire them in a cost-effective manner, then you must reconsider, and abandon, your overall goal in favor of one that is attainable.

This step is the first of several "go-no go" points in the establishment of your firm's marketing plan, a point at which you decide whether what you want to do is feasible.

As you consider the additional skills that are needed to implement your plan, consider also that you can expand your practice without expanding your payroll by forming associations with other firms in the same or different geographical areas. Those firms may offer different services that dovetail with the services your firm offers, or you may be able to refer cases to each other or act as local counsel for each other on certain matters. If you have special expertise in a narrow field of the law, make sure that large firms that may refer cases in that area know of that expertise.

Example: In order to offer prospective clients with medical malpractice claims the best legal representation possible, we need to acquire expertise in the review of medical records and procedures. We will do that by hiring a nurse practitioner to review records on an as-needed basis at a cost of $30 per hour. We will select the nurse practitioner no later than February 1. We must also increase the understanding of the lawyers, paralegals, and clerical staff of medico-legal issues, case law, and terms no later than February 1. Toward that end we will enroll paralegals in the winter "Law & Medicine" seminar offered by the county bar association, lawyers in the winter "Update on Medico-Legal Issues" seminar offered by the ABA, and clerical personnel in the winter community college course "Introduction to medical records." Additionally, we will subscribe to periodicals in the area of legal medicine, join the practice sections of the state bar association and the ABA on legal medicine, and investigate and take advantage of continuing legal education programs that focus on medical malpractice and other medico-legal issues. The law of medical malpractice will become a topic for research and discussion at each firm meeting.

Additional Equipment Required

To reach your goal, you may need to install new equipment, purchase additional software, and purchase new books or online services. Assess the need and the cost and make provisions in your budget to have the new materials on hand when they will be required.

Allow time, also, to become proficient in the use of the new equipment or programs before you or anyone else on staff attempts to use them to meet client needs. If training programs are offered, research the dates on which such programs are available and make plans to have the people who will use the equipment attend.

Again, if the additional required equipment cannot be obtained cost-effectively, abandon the overall goal in favor of one that can be met successfully.

Example: In order to meet our need to provide the highest quality legal representation in the area of legal medicine, we must obtain the software, online services, and books listed below to enable us to conduct research quickly and efficiently in medical as well as legal topics. (List not included)

ANALYZE THE COMPETITION

What other firms offer the same or similar services that you propose to offer? Ask yourself why prospective clients should choose to use your services rather than those of the other firms. And also ask yourself how you might be able to alter the provision of those services to make them unique.

If you wish to offer workers' compensation litigation services, for example, can you assemble a stable of expert witnesses in a variety of medical specialties such as repetitive motion injuries? Or, if you wish to offer estate planning services, is it possible to also offer collateral services, such as tax preparation, to cut down on the number of professionals prospective clients may require to consult with in the future?

Ideally, offer a service that no one else offers. The best way to beat the competition is to plan your attack so that you have none. As Orville Redenbacher advises, pick one thing and do it better than anyone else.

If that's not possible, plan to provide services that better meet the needs of the prospective clients than those provided by the competition.

And take into consideration what opposition the competition might give you in your quest to unseat them or take away a portion of the market share they currently enjoy. They are not apt to sit back quietly as you take potential clients away from them. If they are a much larger firm, you may be in for a battle that, fiscally, is unwinnable.

If that is the case, you might consider approaching the competition with the suggestion that they refer cases in the proposed area that they are unwilling or unable to undertake. Often, cases considered too small a matter for one firm can become the bread and butter for another.

Example: Frank & Thomas is the only other provider of medical malpractice representation in our county. But they also seek to offer a general practice of law, and are not equipped to become expert in all areas. We can meet the competition by concentrating in this area and by becoming known as the firm to engage for malpractice claims. They are unlikely to give up their lucrative estate planning practice to fight for a larger share of the malpractice market.

Analyze the Need for the Proposed Services

You may be able to provide the best possible service in any given area of the law, but your efforts will prove for naught if the marketplace has no need for them.

That may sound simplistic (an admiralty lawyer in Nebraska may be a fish out of water), but in addition to analyzing the competition, you should analyze the marketplace, too, to see if the services you seek to provide meet a need sufficient to justify the expense of offering them.

Also determine whether, and how, the market needs will change in the future. The changes may be detrimental or beneficial, but whatever the changes are, they should be anticipated and planned for.

Example: A new regional medical center is planned to be constructed in the county seat two years from now. That center will increase the number of hospital beds fourfold. The need for concentration in plaintiff medico-legal representation will increase, too. By the time the center is built, our firm should have established a reputation as being the best in the field.

ADVERTISING EFFORTS

What is your target audience and how (if at all) can advertising assist you in meeting your goal?

Once you determine what types of advertising—print, radio, television, direct mail—will have the greatest impact on that audience, and which are permissible within your jurisdiction, select those that are most cost-effective with the help, if necessary, of an agency or counselor.

Choose an advertising strategy that permits you to sustain its drive and one in which different elements are complementary. You would not want to spend your annual advertising budget on one television ad, for example, nor would you want print ads to advertise one service and radio ads another. The result would be to confuse the audience as to what it is you offer, unless the audiences are different and the means of reaching them, the vehicles, are also different.

Example: We will place a quarter-page ad in the Yellow Pages editions to be distributed in Spring, 1996 in our county as well as in those counties that will make up the cachement area for the new regional medical center. We will engage an advertising agency to assist us in developing the ad. Additionally, we will discuss the effect that public service ads, both print and in electronic media, concerning medico-legal issues will have on our future business with the agency, and determine no later than November 1 of this year whether we will utilize them and, if so, to what extent. We will also ask the agency to develop means by which we can track the effectiveness of these ads. We will also investigate the cost and effectiveness of developing or purchasing public service brochures and pamphlets on medico-legal issues for direct mail and as office giveaways no later than November 1 so that, if a decision to use them is made, they can be on hand before the ads appear and will complement the ads.

PUBLIC RELATIONS EFFORTS

What is the public image you want to present? And how can you best present it? The answers to those two questions will determine the public relations efforts you will want to take to assist in positioning your firm in

your community. Much the same as in making decisions about how to use
advertising to your best advantage, you must consider the target audience
you want to reach and the most cost-effective means of reaching it with
your public relations messages. And, much the same as in advertising,
you should consider using a public relations professional to assist you in
developing a plan that is consistent with your advertising initiatives and
that complements them.

The specific steps you take will vary widely according to clientele you
wish to attract.

Example: To complement our advertising program, we will pay for a public
service column in the newspapers of the communities we serve alerting them
to particular problems and issues in medical malpractice. We will engage a
public relations professional to advise when press releases should be prepared
and to prepare them as well. All of these programs will begin in March 1996
or at such other date as the public relations counselor advises.

COMMUNITY RELATIONS EFFORTS

Community relations efforts should also be designed to complement your
advertising and public relations to present a consistent and professional
image of your firm and the services it provides. Again, the type of
community relations program your firm adopts will depend upon the
nature of your practice, but should be designed to be of a more permanent
nature than your advertising and public relations efforts, which may
change more frequently.

A scholarship program, for example, to be effective, should be long-
standing, just as a communitywide people's law school program should be
an annual, if not more frequent, occasion.

Make sure that your public relations and advertising counselors, if you
have retained them, are in on the planning stages for your community
relations program. They will be able to suggest ways for getting valuable
exposure out of it as well.

Example: Our firm will assist in creating a countywide people's law school that
will offer the public at large information on the law in general as well as in our
area of concentration. We will begin planning this initiative immediately to
ensure that it is operational by our overall goal deadline. We will also offer
students at the local school of nursing two $500 scholarships each year with
the competition to begin in the fall of this year. The scholarships will be awarded

in the spring of 1996. We will ask our public relations and advertising counselors to assist us in obtaining maximum positive exposure from these plans.

INTERNAL STAFF TRAINING

In addition to the training that is deemed required to acquire the skills to
provide the proposed services, staff—lawyers, paraprofessionals, clerical,
and others—need to have ongoing training in client-focused programs and
total quality management techniques to increase their productivity and to
enhance client relations.

Your marketing plan must make allowances for this training as well, for
if you fail to meet the client's expectation of quality at any level, your
marketing plan will fail.

Listed in Appendix B are a number of firms, associations, and individuals who can provide training programs and materials available for
your use.

Assess your staff needs for improvement on an ongoing basis, make
client relations problems, and successes, a subject of staff meetings, and
place the priority on service rather than revenues. If your practice serves
a multilingual community, seek training in the languages your clients
speak. Seek specialized training for staff members who need to improve
in specific areas, such as telephone screening if your marketing plan
invites high-volume calls for personal injury consultations. Arrange for all
staff members who have client contact to participate in programs designed
to improve interpersonal relationships. Foster an atmosphere in which
personal growth is encouraged and mistakes are viewed as opportunities
for learning. And empower everyone on staff to make recommendations
for training they feel is needed to help them do their jobs better.

Staff training is perhaps the most important aspect of the marketing
plan, but it is also the most difficult to define, because the needs for
training will be as different from office to office as the personalities and
diverse backgrounds of the people who work there.

Example: All staff members who have client contact will participate in a
three-day retreat conducted by a professional consultant in client relations
scheduled for the first weekend in September. Spouses and children will also
be invited, to make the off-time more enjoyable. Lawyers will attend a sales
seminar in October to learn techniques for improving their abilities to close
and cross-sell services. A writing seminar will be attended by Jack and Sue on

October 3–6 to improve their letter and brief-writing skills. Staff meetings to discuss client-focus and other training needs will be held each Monday morning at 8 o'clock, effective immediately.

CLIENT RELATIONS IMPROVEMENTS

While all the efforts of your marketing plan should be undertaken with the needs and well-being of your clients in mind, you should take special steps to improve client relations. Since effective client relations involve treating them as they would have you treat them, the first step should be to determine how your clients feel you should improve.

In addition to the ongoing dialog that you have with your clients during representation, at the close of matters (or periodically if you handle a large number of matters for a client) ask your clients to assess your performance, both from a transaction-based standpoint (Are you pleased with the result that was obtained?) and from a relationship-based standpoint (Are you pleased with the relationship you had with our firm during our representation?).

Once you obtain the survey results, use them as a basis of discussion during your staff meetings on client relations to identify areas in which you excel (so that effective approaches can be emulated) and areas in which improvements can be suggested and made.

Example: To further our goal of providing client-focused services, we will ask our clients at the close of each matter (or periodically) to frankly assess the manner in which we have represented them and to ask them, in a spirit of cooperation so that we may better prepare to assist them, and others, in the future, for their suggestions for improvement. We will offer them the opportunity to respond anonymously. We will also ask clients during the period of representation to suggest ways in which we could better serve them. This program will begin immediately.

IMPLEMENTING AND TRACKING YOUR EFFORTS

You must monitor the success and shortcomings of each element of your marketing plan as it evolves. By asking for client input, building in tracking mechanisms in your advertising, community relations, and public relations efforts, continually seeking to improve the quality of the services you provide and the skill inventory you must develop to meet your overall goal, using your staff as a resource to pinpoint potential problem areas and make suggestions for change, you will necessarily track the plan's overall performance as it is implemented.

The important consideration is not whether each step works as perfectly as it was envisioned; it won't. One of the purposes of planning is to prepare yourself to meet the unexpected. The consideration is whether you and your staff will remain flexible enough to meet the challenges that will undoubtedly arise and adapt your plan to respond positively to those challenges.

It is that ability, to change with confidence, born of effective planning, that ultimately will determine your success and the success of your firm.

Chapter Eleven

More Than 100 Practical Ways to Get and Keep Clients

Hire Associates Who Can Market

If you have the choice, hire people who will not only make good lawyers, but who can sell the firm by the sheer impact of their presence and demeanor. Give preference to those with special communication skills, sales' experience, or who have been in business for themselves.

Train Partners and Older Associates to Market

Old dogs can be taught new tricks. The client comes first may seem a simple adage, but making it as natural as breathing will take time. Make marketing a subject at all meetings, and include associates in marketing discussions.

Survey Your Clients to Find out Where You Can Improve

Other businesses do it all the time. They know that to keep the competitive edge, they have to find out where they fail to meet customer expectations. So do you. You'll be surprised at how grateful they are that you asked. And don't take "Everything's great" as an answer. Everybody can improve.

Track Your Marketing Efforts

Find out what works by devising a way to track your efforts at gaining new clients and keeping old ones. Use experts in direct mail, advertising, and marketing to help you. It's cheaper in the long run.

Make TQM a Way of Life

Total Quality Management is the wave of the future. It's as applicable to the practice of law as it is to the manufacturing of passenger vans. Read everything there is about it and focus on quality in everything your firm does, from the error-free typing of routine business letters to the preparation for trial of complex litigation matters. Wherever possible, standardize and systematize procedures. Expect and demand the highest quality work product from yourself and others.

High expectations are the key to everything.

Sam Walton

Take a Long Look at Billing Procedures

If necessary, reprogram your automated billings to read like English and make sure that time increments are included line by line. Clients have a right to know whether a phone call to opposing counsel took 5 minutes or 30. If you bill only in 15-minute increments, your client will someday figure out that you're cheating him. Ask clients for suggestions on how to improve your billings. Incorporate their recommendations.

If the Associate Must Tag Along, Bill His Time to Training

If a new associate is along for the ride, to give him or her exposure to a deposition, motion court, or a trial, bill the time for what it is—part of your firm's training program, not the client's. The client comes to you for your expertise, not for your inexperience.

Put the Client First, Always

If you don't know who your boss is, you're in the wrong profession. If your supervisor asks you to do something that would compromise your client, tell him no. It may cost you your job, but it won't cost you your license or your integrity.

The Telephone: It's There for Your Client's Convenience, Not Yours

If you are sitting in your office and you let voice mail screen your calls, you're in the wrong profession, too. Answer your own phone and return all your calls promptly. Return the ones you hate to return first. You'll feel better all day for doing it.

Learn Your Client's Business

It will give you insight into the special problems your client has and make you more able to help. Marketing your services means making yourself more valuable to your client than any other attorney can.

It's better to ask directions twice than get lost once.

Danish proverb

Don't Make Your Client Pay for the Basics

There are firms that charge every photocopy to their clients. That's wrong. Don't charge for the first 10 copies. Then charge a commercially reasonable rate. Don't let the peripheral profit centers become more important than keeping clients. And, be as up-front about nonfee charges as you are about fees.

Get Involved in the Community

Community involvement is good exposure, so long as it's done in noncontroversial areas. Serving on charity boards and fundraising drives gives you the opportunity to do good and rub elbows with VIPs at the same time. But don't solicit business when you're supposed to be doing good works; it sullies your reputation.

Live by the Canons of Ethics

They weren't written as an exercise for smart lawyers to circumvent; they were intended to be the commandments of the profession. Lawyers who live by them are respected. Those who don't end up before hidden cameras on television news magazines.

Use PR Like a Scalpel

It's not how often your name is in print, but for what that counts. You don't want notoriety. You want respect. Save those precious media contacts for releases that are not only newsworthy, but have marketing potential as well. And, while we're on the subject, have a pro write the releases, but make sure the pro does what you want.

Give Seminars for Free, and Invite the Wrong People

Most corporate legal officers, the ones who decide which firms get what business, have been invited to all the seminars they want to see and then some. For a change, arrange a seminar for front-line supervisors or human relations professionals and give them practical guidelines they can use on the job. Serve coffee and doughnuts. The word will trickle up.

A man's judgment is best when he can forget himself and any reputation he may have acquired and can focus wholly on making the right decision.

Admiral Raymond Spruance

If You Must Mail Something, Make It Useful

Glitzy firm brochures with expensive, obviously posed shots of the top partners may look nice, but they end up in the trash can. If you want to send clients something, send them updates on the law that may affect their business, tax tips they can use personally, or other useful information. If you send it in the form of newsletters, use no more than two colors and prepunch them for a three-ring binder.

Fit Your Services to Your Client's Budget

If your client has a $10 problem on a $5 budget, charge him $5. You're $5 ahead of the game and he will remember the bargain you gave him when he has $100 problems on a $50 budget.

Make Everyone a Client Relations Specialist

Give every associate the power to make an adjustment to a client's bill on the spot or the authority to correct other problems, within guidelines, without going higher up. The client wants satisfaction now, not later, and will appreciate the fact that his or her problems were taken care of expeditiously.

Look for Ways to Save Your Client Money and Time

The lawyer who tells a client that his problem can be taken care of without expensive legal fees or protracted litigation will have a client for life. In fact, sometimes a client will accept a result that is less than attractive, but more cost-effective. There really are simple solutions to problems that may seem overwhelming. Seek those solutions first, and you will be regarded as a very wise counselor.

Don't Bill Paralegal Time for Secretarial Work

You wouldn't pay someone $40 an hour to staple multipage pleadings, so why should you expect your client to? Secretarial work is included in your nonbillable overhead. Your client knows that.

> *There is no place in an organization for the overly ambitious person who only looks out for number one. The best way to channel your ambition is to be ambitious—not for yourself—but for your organization. Put all your energies into accomplishing team goals first. After that, all the other things, like your recognition and advancement, will take care of themselves.*
>
> F. A. Manske, *Secrets of Effective Leadership* (Leadership Education and Development, Inc.)

Don't Bill Associate Time for Paralegal Work

Going through mounds of documents received in response to FOIA or discovery requests is something a paralegal can do. Even if a first year associate's billing rate is higher, is it fair to the client to charge the differential?

Bill Flat Rates for Routine Matters

A collection letter is likely to read the same whether an associate, billing at $75 an hour, or a partner, billing at $250 an hour, writes it. Come to think of it, it will read the same if a secretary writes it and the partner or associate merely reviews and signs it. Charge a flat rate for such items.

Don't Gouge, It's Unseemly

Billing two clients for the same hour, eating at a French restaurant rather than having a pizza, placing a surcharge on messenger services or fax transmissions, billing 15 minutes for a 2-minute call, having working lunches where the client pays for the meal as well as the talent, billing clients for the time it takes a partner to make up the billing—you get the idea. In law school, they may have called it fraud.

Travel Only When You Have to, and Then Go Coach

You don't always have to be there. And you don't have to go first class to get there, either. Every unnecessarily spent dollar in legal fees detracts from your client's productivity. Every dollar spent is passed on to your client's customers. If your client's product becomes so expensive it can't compete in the marketplace, the client's business fails. You lose a client. In the final analysis, the back of the airplane gets there almost as soon as the nose.

Do Good Deeds Occasionally

It makes you feel good. That makes you happier. Being happier makes you more productive on the job. You serve your client better.

No one ever excused himself to success.

David Del Dotto

Call Yourself Up

Want an eye-opener? Call your firm someday when you're out of town. Pretend to be a potential client and ask to speak to yourself. You'll know how the support staff comes across by the time you're through. Ask tough questions, like "Who's the expert in bankruptcy?" and "Is he a good lawyer?"

Encourage Associates to Bring in New Clients

It doesn't matter if they bring in nickel-and-dime business. They will feel as though they are contributing. Compliment them on their resourcefulness and they'll continue to bring in new business. Someday, they might surprise you with what they bring in.

Benchmark Other Service Providers

You know about benchmarking. Identify the best in class in providing a service that you provide, meet with them and find out how they do what they do so well, and emulate their procedures. In grade school, we called it copying off another's paper. But it's legal. The Ford Taurus has more than 200 features that were copied from other cars, according to *Fortune* magazine. If you have an area in your firm that isn't as good as it could be—in billing, secretarial, accounting, wherever—give benchmarking a try.

Make Marketing Part of Your Firm's CLE Requirement

Continuing legal education is sometimes seen as a pain in the neck, but it's important to your ability to provide your clients with advice and service that is competent. If you don't make marketing your firm's services just as important, you won't have to worry about continuing ed.

Don't Shoot from the Hip

It takes one shot from the hip that misses the mark by a mile to forever brand you in your client's eyes as a liar and an idiot. Your client is likely an intelligent human being, aware (perhaps painfully) that you do not have the answer to all of the problems of the universe on the tip of your tongue. When you don't know the answer, say so. Then find the answer and report back. It worked in the army; it will work for you.

> *The people with whom you gossip [in the workplace] will always distrust you, because they well know you may dish them next.*
>
> Ben Stein, *Glamour Magazine*

Team Up for Special Projects

When a client's problems are multifaceted, make use of the talent your firm has in different specialties. Consider the creation of ad hoc problem-solving teams to tackle problems that involve more than your own area of concentration. It saves research time and covers all the bases for your client.

Say Thank You

When a client gives you work, thank her. When you complete the work, thank her. She could just as easily take her work somewhere else, so be grateful that she has decided to entrust it to you.

Brainstorm

If you think there is no better way to accomplish a task, brainstorm with your colleagues. With the only hard and fast rule being that no one can say anything negative about another's idea, you'll be surprised at the creativity that flows in a brainstorming session. Try this question for a starter: "What one thing a month can each lawyer in the firm do to improve relationships with his clients?"

Make Pro Bono Work a Requirement

It reminds you of what being a lawyer is all about: helping people. Besides, it makes you a better person. Volunteer to be a guardian ad litem for abused kids, or represent the indigent.

If you think you can, or think you can't, you're probably right.

Mark Twain

Do Your Homework Before You Meet with a New Client

Your client will appreciate it if you take the time to understand his business needs and the problems of his industry. Request copies of and read his annual reports. Have your secretary research magazine articles and newspaper clips on his company. Pretend you're going on a job interview, because you are.

Give Your Clients Choices

When your research indicates that there is more than one possible solution to a client's problem, give her the options in writing, detailing the benefits and detriments, as well as the estimated costs in time and money. If you wish, recommend the one that you feel is best, but let her choose the course of action she feels suits her needs best. Clients like to think that they have had a share in creating the solution.

Treat New Clients Like Start-Ups

A start-up business is concerned about the bottom line. When you start with a new client, give him cost projections so that he will know what he's getting into. Tailor your approach to his problems with his resources in mind. Never tell him he can't afford the services you can deliver, but make sure you offer him only what he can pay for without sacrificing his company's profitability. Help your client's business grow, and you'll have a client for life.

Remember, Financial Success Isn't a Goal, It's a By-Product

Take your sights off making a lot of money. The target is providing the highest quality legal services you can. Focus on that and that alone. The money will come later. If money is the focus, the quality of the service will diminish.

Measure Everything

To improve quality, you have to have adequate ways to measure the work you do. In a machine shop, they do it with micrometers, to make sure that tolerances are uniformly within specifications. In a law firm, you might measure the accuracy of citations, individual lawyers' "kill" rates in motion court, the way in which jurors perceive the effectiveness of your litigators, the number of articles your firm is able to strategically place in publications, the way in which your receptionist answers the telephone, the quality of your fax transmissions. Everything that can be measured should be, and if it can be improved, then improve it and measure it again. Quality is a goal you will always strive for and never reach.

> *Success isn't making a better mousetrap or even a million. Success is much more personal than that. It's meeting the goals you set for yourself.*
>
> Me

Forget Organization Charts

Organization charts stifle creativity. First year associates know more law than partners and their inventiveness has not yet been squeezed out of them. They should be included in planning sessions and encouraged to contribute. And, just like in the brainstorming sessions, never treat an idea from anyone with ridicule. He will never give you another.

Make Performance Reviews Useful

When you review the performance of a subordinate, mention the billable hours, but don't focus on them alone. If criticism is necessary, be sure to criticize the work and not the person. Compliment the lawyer in areas in which she is strong and make suggestions for improvement in areas where she is weak. Help the individual set definite goals for improvement and set times to meet in the future to review progress. By making the performance review a positive training event, you are preparing for your firm's future.

Use Your Time Better

Every morning, make a list with three columns: Must Do, Should Do, and Might Do. Focus on the must dos first. When they're done, turn your attention to the should dos. If you have time left over, tackle the might dos. Use your travel time to catch up on professional reading, reviewing notes and case files, and writing correspondence. Buy some motivational tapes on marketing and listen to them on your car's stereo system while you drive. Every unused moment is an opportunity for self-improvement.

Learn to Write

Often, your client will judge your effectiveness as a lawyer by the effectiveness of your correspondence, and your intelligence by your spelling and adherence to the rules of grammar. Ask your public relations team to give you a frank appraisal of your writing and make the effort to improve in areas of weakness. There are a number of good books on business writing at your local library, too. By improving your communication skills, you improve the image of your firm.

Try these books: *Writing Effectively for Business,* by Sandra Smythe and Beth Neman (Harper Collins); *Put It in a Memo: A Practical Guide to Persuasive Business Writing,* by Helen Gorenstein (Houghton Mifflin); and *Effective Business Communication: The Complete Guide to Business Correspondence,* by Laura Chesterton (Houghton Mifflin).

Help the New Hires

There was a partner I once knew who enjoyed seeing new lawyers stumble and fall their first times in court. I'm sure he thought they were paying their dues. What he didn't see was the impression it made on others. They didn't see a new lawyer. They saw a lawyer from a particular law firm. The law firm's image was sullied, too. That's poor marketing. Help new lawyers to do their best. It makes you look good, too.

The best single way to make sure you delegate well is to stress results more than methods.

Raymond O. Loen, *Manage More*
By Doing Less (McGraw Hill)

Give Credit Where Credit's Due

People are more productive when they are happy where they work. Create an atmosphere of teamwork by recognizing a colleague's achievements with a short, handwritten note or a card. If an associate has helped with a case, mention his or her name in a letter to the client and make sure the associate gets a copy. Giving recognition for a job well done makes people more willing to work with you in the future.

Clients Belong to the Firm, Not the Partner

There's no room for jealousy in a law firm. Partners who guard their clients from other partners are cheating their clients out of the opportunity to give more work to the firm. Attorneys no more own clients than your druggist owns you.

Say Nothing to a Newspaper Reporter, Less to a TV Reporter

Unprepared, flip comments on the courthouse steps may make you feel important for an instant, but the way they're edited and appear in print or on the six o'clock news may be a source of embarrassment for your firm and your client. Think of the media as a tool for your use. Use it the way you would use any tool: very carefully, and only for the right job.

Don't Resist Change

As the business world changes, your client's needs change. Your firm must be amenable to change, too, if it is to remain competitive. Greet changes as opportunities for improving services, even when you don't agree with them. To make dealing with change more palatable, involve others in finding ways to implement the changes, share information about all aspects of the changes openly, and let subordinates freely discuss their fears about the effects the changes may have on them.

Be a Builder

Part of your job, whether you're the newest associate or the oldest partner, is to build your firm's intangible assets: its knowledge, the confidence and trust it not only enjoys, but has in others as well, its commitment to its purpose or ideal, its efficiency, its flexibility and creative sense, its shared attitude of teamwork, and its image in the community. [From William C. Waddell in *Overcoming Murphy's Law* (AMACOM)]

> *Sandwich every bit of criticism between two layers of praise.*
>
> Mary Kay Ash, *Mary Kay on People Management*

Have Confidence in Your Associates' Abilities

If you let an associate know that she has the ability to get a difficult task done, she will work to meet your expectation. Conversely, if your expectations are low, the work product will reflect those dim views. Make your expectations high, have faith in your colleagues' abilities, and let them do their jobs with a minimum of supervision if you want to unlock their potential.

Don't Drink at Lunch

It looks bad, dulls your perceptions, and interferes with your ability to interact with clients and coworkers. Don't do it.

Don't Overdress

If you want to make a fashion statement, do it on your own time, not your firm's. What you are in the business of selling is your legal and political acumen, not sartorial splendor. Overdressing detracts from the image that you want to project of a serious and competent professional.

Suggest Nontraditional Ways to Solve Your Client's Problems

Sometimes a client comes to you with a problem that, at best, is quasi-legal. If a solution that doesn't involve the use of your services is apparent to you, mention it to the client. By helping him with a problem that doesn't involve legal fees, you add to your reputation as a counselor and a friend who is interested in more than fees.

Remember You're the Servant

Never treat a client with less than absolute respect. You are his servant and he can have you dismissed in the blink of an eye. Never speak down to her. She knows her business as well as, if not better than, you know yours.

You are selling advice, and, if you look out your window, you will see that there are more than half a million other purveyors of that commodity in the United States today.

There are three conditions that should exist before you argue at work. They are: The problem should be a permanent one; The problem should be serious; and, You should have a real chance to win.

William A. Delaney, in *Effective Communication on the Job,* edited by William K. Fallon (AMACOM)

Get Your Firm to Sponsor a Little League Team

It's fun. It builds relationships with parents from a variety of backgrounds. Your firm's name, emblazoned on the uniform backs, will get positive exposure. And kids will grow up thinking your firm is composed of something more than lawyers. It's building for the future.

Say "We"

Too much use of the first person singular limits a client's opportunity to become involved in the conversation. It's demeaning to pay someone $200 an hour and then be forced to listen to him pontificate on his virtues, skills, knowledge, and abilities. Think "we." The problem your client has is one you share. Make him feel that he is an active participant in all the decisions that are made. The more you think "we," the more you and your client become a team.

Get Work Done "Just in Time"

Industry focuses on making sure that work is completed "just in time" for the next phase to begin. It's no different in a law firm. You have deadlines to meet. Two tips: 1. When promising a client when she can expect work to be completed, add a day to your best estimate. Then complete the work early and get it to her before the agreed-upon deadline. 2. Always schedule time for unexpected delays, illnesses, etc. You'll look like a wizard for getting the job done despite the blizzard of '96.

A Word about Voice Mail

Voice mail saves money and secretarial time. But it can be terribly annoying to a client. Avoid the transfer loop problem, where callers are subjected to recording after recording, trying to find a live human being to talk to. And if your recording says that you're "on another line or have just stepped out of the office," make sure you change it at night or when you go to the beach for two weeks. Your client will assume you just don't want to talk to him.

Tell Clients the Why of Things

He has a right to know what he's buying with his hard-earned money. You may think you know what's right for him, but that assumption is just as apt to be wrong. Tell clients not only what you recommend, but why. And make sure they understand so there are no disappointments later.

The quality of a man's life is in direct proportion to his commitment to excellence.

Vince Lombardi

Read Trade Magazines

Trade magazines often project trends and potential pitfalls in your client's industry. By keeping up on what's new in her business world, you'll be better prepared to discuss those problems with her and take preventive action when needed.

Ask to Take a Tour of Your Client's Business

Get to know some of the people you may have to deal with and get a feel for what your client's world is all about. He will appreciate the interest and your desire to learn about what the most important thing in his life is. Being able to visualize how his work is done will save time in future meetings, too, by eliminating questions.

Use the Least Expensive Discovery Tools

A deposition, taken on the opposite coast, can be very expensive to your client. If a request for admission would do the same job for the price of a stamp, why not try it. Look for ways to save your client money in the discovery process and file motions only when you really need to. Act as though you are the faithful steward of your client's litigation war chest.

Offer Your Client a Copy of Everything

Most clients don't want to see copies of every pleading, memo, letter, etc. But they should have the choice. Often, such papers are the only tangible evidence of the work you do, and it's what they are paying for. If the client requests copies, make sure they're legible and presented with as much care as your bill.

Become Involved with Your Alumni Association

You can make many valuable professional and business contacts by becoming active in the alumni affairs of your law school and undergraduate college. It is also an opportunity to get free publicity in their magazines, some of which have circulations that rival commercial periodicals.

Dreams and dedication are a powerful combination.

William Longgood,
Voices From The Earth (Norton)

Get Involved in Local Politics

Another way to garner free and favorable publicity is to become involved in local politics, such as service on the school board of your municipality. If you have a desire to enter politics on a larger scale, have a trusted associate give you a frank assessment of what the press could reveal about your personal and professional affairs. More than one career has been destroyed in the heat of a political campaign.

Get Involved in Professional Organizations and Practice Sections

Develop a high profile in your area of concentration by becoming active in professional organizations (engineering for patent attorneys, for example), your county and state bar associations, and practice sections of the American Bar Association. Attorneys in other areas of concentration will become aware of your abilities, a must for case referral and consulting activities.

Develop or Hire Expertise Where It's Needed

If your local market has a need for an attorney who is a specialist in some arcane area of the law, either have someone on staff develop the requisite expertise or hire an attorney who has it. Find niches that need filling and fill them.

Look into Hiring Successful Solo Practitioners

Law firms traditionally don't look at solo practitioners as a market for talent for hire, but consider this: solo practitioners survive (and some do very well) because they have the demonstrated ability to market their services. They already possess the skills you are trying to develop.

Avoid Unethical Lawyers

Do not associate, publicly or privately, with lawyers who are unethical or you suspect are engaged in unlawful activity. If you have a lawyer in your firm who falls into one of these categories, get rid of him or her before the firm's reputation suffers.

> *The effectiveness of your life is measured by the effectiveness of your communication.*
>
> Earl Nightingale

Publish in Your Area of Concentration

Another way to get favorable publicity for your firm is to encourage partners and associates to publish in their respective areas. Have paralegals check citations for accuracy and professional writers edit the material if necessary. Submit material to trade and professional periodicals. Avoid op-ed writing, unless undertaken on behalf of a client.

Strive to Become the Expert in Your Field

Experts never have to look for work; they attract it. By constantly seeking self-improvement, information in your field, and excellence in the practice of your specialty, you will one day become an expert in it. Make it a habit to devote some time each day to study.

Teach at a Local College or Law School

Besides being a thoroughly enjoyable avocation, teaching as an adjunct professor keeps you sharp, makes you practice oral presentation skills, and gives you the opportunity to meet young people who, if you do your job right, will regard you as a source of information and wise counsel when they are in business.

Never Discuss One Client with Another

There are attorneys who discuss one client's personality traits or affairs in the presence of another, perhaps to indicate that they have more than one client. The client they are talking to, however, is smart enough to know that the lawyer can't be trusted to keep a confidence. Consider even the fact that a client comes to you for advice as confidential information, and never disclose the fact of the relationship in an effort to gain new business without the client's permission.

Make a List of Those Whose Skill in Marketing You Admire

Whether they are lawyers or not, they are people you can learn from. Keep the list short, and try to get together as a group once a month for lunch to share ideas and strategies. Ask them for their secrets, and share your thoughts with them.

> *Those who don't value what they do will never be successful at it. Those who don't enjoy their work will ultimately fail.*
>
> Richard Germann

Refer Cases out of Your Area of Concentration

If you have a case your firm lacks the expertise to handle, refer it to an acknowledged expert in the field. In the cover letter, remind him or her of the areas of the law in which your firm is particularly adept. Referrals generally work both ways. Never request or accept a referral fee.

Avoid Conflicts Like the Plague

Review your procedures for determining whether you would have a conflict of interest in accepting a new matter or a new client. For corporate clients, find out the names of subsidiaries and joint venture partners.

When in doubt, obtain the permission of both old and new clients before continuing.

Resolve Client Disputes

When you have a dispute with a client, how is it resolved? To ensure fairness, and avoid litigation, offer to employ the services of an impartial mediator, if all other attempts to satisfy the client fail. Then abide by the mediator's decision. Never let a client leave with unresolved anger if you can prevent it.

Join Civic Groups

Join civic groups such as the Chamber of Commerce, Rotary, and Kiwanis. Invite the heads of new businesses to their luncheon meetings. It's not soliciting, and it can give you an edge, providing you never initiate discussions on legal representation.

Start a Scholarship Fund

For favorable publicity you could never buy for the same investment, start a scholarship fund for students with tremendous potential from disadvantaged backgrounds. Someday they will be in business, and they will never forget your help. Nor will the community. You might consider asking leaders in business to help you make the selections from essays, profiles, and so forth. Involvement in common good works creates binding relationships.

> *Progress always involves risk; you can't steal second base and keep your foot on first.*
>
> Frederick Wilcox

Never Publicize Salaries

The starting salaries of associates and the salaries of partners are private matters and deserve to be treated as such. Many of the direct contacts you have at client companies don't make as much, and they may be less willing to overlook small errors made by people with less experience than those who make more money.

Check Your Business Card

If it doesn't have your home telephone number on it, you're telling your client that you are only accessible during business hours. Sometimes, needs arise at inopportune times. Be available. (A lawyer who read this one said it's fine for business clients, but not for divorce or criminal clients. I disagree. People going through the most troubling of times have the greatest need for the counseling aspect of your job. The National Institute of Health has recently listed domestic violence as the most frequent cause of death in young women. If one telephone call to a rational mind at three in the morning could save one life, it's worth losing a little sleep over.)

Quality Is Your Problem

Hire consultants to train your people, if you wish, but the day-to-day monitoring of your quality program must be done by you. If you rely on outsiders to do it, it won't get done.

Follow It up in Writing

If a client asks for advice, follow up your verbal advice with a letter. It serves two purposes. First, you have a chance to review what you said. If it's still valid, fine; if not, call the client back immediately. Second, advice in writing is less likely to be misunderstood.

Calculate Your Client's Worth

How much is each client worth to you on an annual basis? How about for 5 years, or 10? Take time to figure it out. It will make a difference in how you treat them on a daily basis.

Good counselors lack no clients.

Shakespeare

Keep up with Technology

Changes in technology are often opportunities for providing additional, nonlegal services for your client. A recent innovation in combining video tapes and CD ROMs, for example, makes the instant retrieval of footage of construction project inspections a reality. In future litigation, this easily stored information would be of great value to your client.

Become Your Client's Partner

View your relationship with your client as symbiotic. As the client's business grows, so does yours. You must be able to offer business advice as well as legal advice to survive in this market.

Advertise Wisely

Plan the use of your advertising dollars. Select the audience you want to reach first. Then determine the message you want to send to them. Finally, select the medium that will take the message to the audience in the most direct and cost-efficient manner. The most expensive form of advertising is not always the most effective.

Try the New Approach

Don't waste time worrying if a new approach to a problem will fail. If you wait too long, it will; it will die of old age. Don't be afraid to be on the cutting edge or to follow your gut instinct about what to do. That's being a leader. Sure, you'll screw up, and maybe you should charge less when you do, but with every victory you become more of an asset to your client.

On Hiring Support Personnel . . .

If you're going to hire a new secretary, put the best secretary you have on the hiring committee. Her input will be more important than yours. Same goes for hiring paralegals; your best paralegal will know which applicant will be the best player on your team.

. . . And Once They're Hired

Once hired, let them see where their work ends up: give them a glimpse of the big picture. In one company, assembly line workers cut electrical cable into 10-foot lengths, eight hours a day, day in and day out. Morale was horrible. Then their foreman took them to the obstetrical unit of a local hospital and showed them the fetal heart monitors their cables powered. When they realized the importance of their work, morale—and productivity—increased.

Become International

If your corporate clients (or potential clients) conduct business overseas, you have to, too. That doesn't mean you have to establish an office over there, though. But it does mean that you should establish relationships with the offices of lawyers who practice in the countries where your client does business. Being able to say, "We also have a correspondent relationship with the firm of O'Malley, O'Malley & O'Rourke" would be a plus for you if your client does business in Dublin. (You can become "national" the same way, by developing relationships with firms in other cities.)

Set Goals for Everything

To improve your performance, set goals, measurable performance objectives that have deadlines, for every task. According to Organizational Dynamics, the mere setting of a goal has positive effects.

Plans are nothing. Planning is everything.

Dwight D. Eisenhower

Treat the Court Reporter Nicely

When you're at a deposition and opposing counsel leaves the room, does the court reporter ever make a flip, derogatory comment about him or her, or make a gesture, for example, roll his eyes or shrug? They'll do the same about you even if your client is still sitting at the table when you excuse yourself, if you make their lives difficult. Court reporters have also been known to recommend attorneys.

People's Law Schools

If your community doesn't already have a people's law school, an event sponsored by local bar associations in which local attorneys and judges present up-to-date, informative sessions for the public and answer questions, start one. If your community has one, get involved in it.

Public Television

Sponsor programs on your local PBS station. You might consider providing the funding for a series of movies concerning the practice of law, including such films as *Inherit the Wind, To Kill a Mockingbird,* and *Young Mr. Lincoln.*

Make Your Waiting Room Work for You

Don't pile the coffee table in your waiting room high with legal journals. Instead, subscribe to magazines and journals that will appeal to your clients' interests, such as trade and professional periodicals in their fields. If yours is a general practice, let the selection reflect the broad range of the services you provide. Some offices effectively use brief videotapes to inform their clients on changes in the law, making the waiting room experience a learning one.

And make sure clients are warmly greeted and made comfortable upon their arrival. If there is to be an unexpected delay and you were unable to inform the client of it before they left to see you, tear yourself away from whatever it is that caused the delay, apologize, and give the client a definite time when you will be able to tend to his or her needs. In no event should it be more than 10 minutes.

1–800 Numbers

If your practice is a national one, invest in a 1–800 line. It says that you are trying to find ways in which to save your clients money. (You can also get state and/or regional 1–800 numbers.)

Consistent, high quality service boils down to two equally important things: caring and competence.

> Chip R. Bell and Ron Zemke,
> *Service Wisdom*

Charitable Donations

Studies have shown that firms that donate to charities generate goodwill. To make the goodwill last a little longer, consider donating to building projects, such as hospital rooms and library carrels, where a bronze plaque will remind others of your generosity for years to come.

Law Day

Sponsor an essay or coloring contest for local school students on Law Day. Give $100, $50, and $25 US Savings Bonds as prizes. Your cost will be less than $100, but think of the publicity you will generate!

Brand Loyalty

If a client comes to your firm because of the reputation of a particular lawyer, make sure that lawyer deals with the client. Associates and other partners may work on the file, but the face-to-face client contact should be by the lawyer hired by the client.

Bumper Stickers and Vanity Plates

If your car sports a bumper sticker that promotes a political or social issue, consider whether it alienates a substantial number of potential clients who support the other side. Vanity license plates that are too cute can make you look foolish or self-important. In one state, a college professor has a plate that reads, "Me Prof." Hopefully, he doesn't teach English.

TV Ads

Public service ads that help the public, rather than hype your firm, can be very effective. What you *don't* say is often more important than what you *do*. Imagine the impact of an ad in which a personal injury lawyer asks people to wear their seat belts: "Put me out of a job. Buckle up."

> *You can tell more about a person by what he says about others than you can by what others say about him.*
>
> Dale Carnegie

Other Professionals

Develop relationships with people in other professions, such as accounting, medicine, insurance, real estate sales, funeral home management, engineering, and business. Everyone you meet has the power to refer cases to you and to speak well of you to others.

Be Enthusiastic

As I was writing the above tip, a young woman from Federal Express rang my doorbell and delivered a package to me. Before I could say anything, she flashed a broad smile and said "Good morning!" with true enthusiasm. I thanked her for the delivery, and she said, "You don't have to thank me. I love doing my job." Says a lot about Federal Express, doesn't it?

Do the Right Thing

Nordstrom Industries, a leader in sales, has the shortest employee handbook in the world: "Use your good judgment in all situations. There will be no additional rules."

In management, the cliche is, "Managers do things right; leaders do the right thing."

Doing the right thing says a lot about you.

Mock Trials Shouldn't End in Law School

Use the resources at your disposal to pretry important cases in front of "jurors." Let new associates practice arguments and interrogation techniques in front of seasoned trial lawyers. Train. Train. Train. And when you're through, start the cycle over again. We "practice" law because it can never be mastered.

Encourage Self-Improvement

As you ask your clients to tell you whether you're giving them the quality representation that they expect, you should ask every person in your firm whether you can improve the ways in which you meet their needs. At first, they will be hesitant to respond, but if you can get them to suggest ways in which the firm can improve, you've started a revolution.

Encourage all to request help in improving their skills, whatever they are, and then meet those needs. If you fail to do your best to me the requested needs of even one person, you will never be trusted again.

Self-improvement is contagious, and once it's started, it becomes a habit.

You can attract a lot more flies with honey than you can with vinegar.

My Mother

More on Business Cards

You have business cards. So do your paralegals. If you want everyone else on the staff of your firm to feel a sense of ownership, give them cards that say Client Relations. It also reminds them what the most important part of their job is.

Recognition Is Crucial

If you have a firm Christmas party/dinner or a summer cookout, or anytime EVERY person in the firm is together for fun, use that time to give awards for service. Just about everyone should get something, a plaque, a certificate, whatever, to show how much the firm values their individual contributions. Stars should get more, but remember that there are star clerks, secretaries, paralegals, messengers, receptionists, and typists, too.

Call Waiting

What you say: "Just a second, I have another call."

What the client hears: "Just a second, I have another call that may be more important than yours."

Wasted Time Can Be Productive Time

The receptionist who spends time between answering calls and greeting visitors thumbing through popular magazines or reading novels is wasting her time, and yours. Get her involved in the business of your practice. Have her thumb through trade, business, and professional magazines and newspapers. The good news she finds about clients should be passed on to the responsible attorney. A quick congratulatory note to the client will be greatly appreciated. (Thank the receptionist for the information, too.)

This One Gets Everyone Thinking

In *A Passion For Excellence* (Random House), Tom Peters and Nancy Austin write about a firm named Markem in Keene, New Hampshire. The firm produces its own yearly calendar for their employees' use. The quotes that pepper the calendar are "a full year of quality thoughts from

Markem employees to inspire our finest performance," according to the calendar's cover.

Client relations isn't an adjunct to your job, it's a very real and very large part of your job.

Me

And Finally . . .

Speak and write in English. I knew a young lawyer—graduated at the top of his class—who alienated the blue-collar segment of his client base by talking as though he were a law professor. No one was impressed. In fact, they took it as an insult. Remember, the reason for speech and written communications is to be understood.

Appendix A
Your Law

Get It in Writing

Test your legal knowledge. Which of the parties below should consider drafting a written contract?

Scene 1: Cynthia and Eric plan to marry in a few months. Some years ago, Cynthia inherited a cottage on the lake from her grandmother. She tells Eric that she wants it to remain hers alone no matter what happens in the future. Eric readily agrees.

Scene 2: Jerry has a daughter, Linda, a free-lance writer who recently married Chuck. Linda and Chuck tell Jerry they've found a house they want to buy, but their bank is uncertain whether they will be able to afford the mortgage. Will he please guarantee their loan from the bank? Jerry responds that he is more than willing to help out but that he will expect to be paid back if he ever does have to make a mortgage payment for them.

Scene 3: Tim wants to buy his neighbor Alice's year-old Porsche. He offers her a fair price, but goes on to explain that because he's experiencing a "temporary cash-flow problem" he'd like her to give him the keys now in exchange for his promise to pay her off over the next five years. Alice is experiencing a cash-flow problem herself, so she tells him it's a deal.

Often all you need to form a binding legal contract is an oral offer, a voluntary acceptance of that offer, and the exchange of some bargained-for benefit or performance between the parties (consideration). But in almost every case (including the above examples) the safer practice is to put your agreement in writing and see that it is signed by both parties.

Let's review some general principles. Although the requirements vary from state to state, contracts usually need to be in writing and signed in order to be enforceable in court if they include:

- any promise to be responsible for someone else's debts (a surety contract);
- any promise to bequeath property to someone;
- any promise involving a change in ownership of land or an interest in land (such as a lease);
- any promise for the sale of goods worth more than $500;
- any promise that, from the outset, the parties cannot possibly fulfill within one year from when they make the promise.

Other contracts may also need to be in writing, and oral contracts are more likely to lead to disputes even when they are enforceable. A written contract can head off later misunderstandings by giving each party a chance to read and understand every term before agreeing to it. And if a dispute does arise, pointing to a clearly written contract is the easiest way to prove its terms.

continued on page 2

IN THIS ISSUE

Home Improvement Contracts:
Think Before You Sign

Now that it's spring, many home-owners are getting the urge to do something about their dingy kitchens, sagging gutters, or too-small closets. But who should you pick to do the job? Although most contractors are honest and conscientious, you should choose carefully.

The Federal Trade Commission, federal truth-in-lending laws, and state deceptive practices laws all play a part in protecting you when you hire someone to make home repairs. It's the law: Home repair contractors may not mislead you in order to get the job.

Keeping in mind that it's important to maintain good relations with your contractor and to avoid souring that relationship by inadvertently implying that he or she is out to fleece you, you should nonetheless be wary of contractors who:

- promise a lower price for allowing your home to be used as a model or to advertise their work (Has the price really been lowered? What does the "use of your home" entail?);

- provide free gifts (What exactly are the gifts? When will you receive them? Can you get a price reduction instead?).

Avoid contractors who:
- leave delivery and installation costs out of their estimates;
- offer to give you a rebate or referral fee if any of your friends use the same contractor;
- promised other homeowners better materials than they actually used;
- insist on starting work before you sign a contract;
- claim that your house is dangerous and needs immediate repair (unless you know it does);
- claim to work for a government agency.

The best way to protect yourself is to get written estimates from several contractors. Be sure to describe the job to each prospective contractor in exactly the same way, so they all bid on the same job. Also ask friends and neighbors what they have paid recently for the kind of work you want done, and ask the contractor to give you the names and phone numbers of people for whom he or she has recently worked. Check out the contractor with the Better Business Bureau.

Unless there are unusual circumstances and little money is involved, don't allow any work to begin until there's a signed contract. Even then, be wary of signing a contract that reads simply "work as per agreement." The contract should contain a complete description of all the work to be done, who will do it, the materials to be used, the appliances and fixtures to be supplied, the dates for starting and completing the job, and a provision about cleanup of the premises. Watch out for disclaimers of responsibility for the quality of work or materials.

The contract also should detail all charges, including finance charges, if any. The total labor cost should be broken down into the hourly rates on which the cost is based, including carpenter's rate, electrician's rate, and so on. If the contractor guarantees the work for a particular period of time, this also should be stated in the contract.

Under federal and some state laws you may have a three-day "cooling off" period in which to cancel con-*continued on page 4*

Get It in Writing
continued from page 1

Now let's take another look at our three scenarios.

Scene 1: Cynthia's cottage on the lake probably would still be in her sole possession upon her marriage to Eric, since the laws of most states consider property held at the time of marriage as separate. So why have a written contract? Because over time, Cynthia's separate property will not necessarily remain her separate property, nor will it necessarily be free from later claims by Eric or his creditors.

For example, in some states Eric might have a claim to the cottage if the couple adds a bathroom to it, or pays the taxes on the property out of their joint checking account, or rents it out occasionally and deposits the income in their joint account. And if Cynthia and Eric ever divorce, the courts in some states would have the power to award the cottage to Eric, either as part of the division of marital property or to provide him with support. In some states the increase in the cottage's value over the years of their marriage could belong to both spouses in equal shares.

Therefore, depending on the value of the cottage and on how important it is to the couple to do everything they can to ensure that Cynthia will retain sole ownership, they might want to consider drafting a premarital contract well before their wedding date. This document should state the couple's intention to marry, describe the property, and spell out what happens if it increases in value or if both Eric and Cynthia pay for its upkeep.

Scene 2: As already noted, a surety contract (such as Jerry's promise to be responsible for Linda and Chuck's mortgage payments) generally must be in writing to be enforceable. The bank will insist on it.

But what about Linda and Chuck's agreement to pay Jerry back if he ever has to make a mortgage payment for them? Because Jerry will have to honor his legal obligation to the bank regardless of whether Chuck and Linda honor their promise to him, he may want to make sure the couple understands that he intends to treat their oral promise as a legal obligation. The clearest way to manifest that intention is to put their private understanding into writing.

Scene 3: Similarly, Alice should put her agreement with Tim in writing—her Porsche is surely worth more than $500. While she's at it, Alice should outline exactly how she wants to be paid: How much should each payment be? When should payments be made? What happens if Tim falls behind in his payments?

Remember, it's important not only to get your agreement in writing, but also to make sure that it clearly spells out all of the terms of the agreement.

2

In the Child's Best Interests

During the 1980s, the faces of missing children began to confront us from billboards, the backs of truck trailers, and even milk cartons. Some of these children have been kidnapped, others have run away from home, but many missing children have been snatched by a parent (or someone working with a parent) who is willfully violating a custody order.

Attitudes toward custody have changed a great deal over the decades. Until the middle of the 19th century, fathers had a nearly absolute right to retain custody of their children. This attitude began to change in the late 1800s, until by the 1970s courts almost always awarded custody of "children of tender years" to their mothers.

Now courts in most states decide custody based on the best interests of the children. What does this mean for parents disputing custody of their children? Here are the answers to some of the most frequently asked questions:

Q. What is child custody?

A. It is the right and duty to care for a child on a day-to-day basis and to make major decisions about the child.

Q. What does sole custody mean?

A. The law assumes that a person with sole custody of a child will have the child live with him or her most of the time and will make major decisions about the child, such as where

he or she goes to school, where the child lives, whether to get braces, etc.

Q. How do courts decide which parent gets custody?

A. In most states, courts decide custody based on the child's best interests, without preferring either mothers or fathers. Unwed parents also have a right to claim custody.

Q. What determines the best interests of the child?

A. When assigning custody, courts often consider the child's wishes. Other factors include the child's relationship with each parent, siblings, and other family members who greatly affect his or her life. The child's physical and educational needs are weighed, as well as the permanence and continuity of the proposed custodial home, the parent's willingness to foster the child's continuing relationship with the non-custodial parent, and the mental, physical, and financial health of everyone involved.

Q. Do some factors outweigh others in awarding custody?

A. In most states, stability and the fitness of the custodial parent weigh more heavily than other factors.

Q. What is joint custody?

A. It can mean joint legal custody, joint physical custody, or both.

Q. What is joint legal custody?

A. When parents agree to joint legal custody, or when a court orders it, they must share major decisions

about their child. Many states require parents to specify which decisions they will share, such as major decisions regarding health or education. Most of these states also order parents to indicate the process they will use if they disagree. Many parents agree to mediate or go to private arbitration before resorting to the courts to settle their differences.

Q. What is joint physical custody?

A. It is a legal arrangement in which the child lives in the homes of both parents. It does not necessarily mean that the child spends equal time in each home, but it does require both parents to maintain a "real" home for the child, who usually has his or her own bedroom. Often the child spends some school nights in each home, and goes to day care or school directly from both homes.

Q. How does joint physical custody affect child support?

A. In most states, the amount of custodial time spent with each parent and the parents' incomes are factors in determining the allocation of child support, but joint custody does not necessarily mean that a parent will not have to pay child support.

Q. Can child custody decisions be changed?

A. Yes. A court can always change child custody arrangements to meet the changing needs of the growing child and to respond to changes in the parents' lives. A court keeps its jurisdiction over the case as long as the child is under the age of majority. When a parent seeks to change a child's custody, the court usually requires the parent to show that conditions have changed greatly since the last order and that changing the custody arrangement will be better for the child.

Q. What is child snatching?

A. This form of kidnapping occurs when a parent or someone working with the parent disobeys a court's custody order by taking or keeping a child away from the other parent.

Q. What happens if the parent takes the child out of state?

A. State and federal laws now require all states to uphold lawful custody decrees made in other states. These laws provide for the return of the child to the custodial parent without the need for a court order. Further custody proceedings are held in the home state.

3

Reservations About the Friendly Skies

You might think that the boarding pass you've had in your desk drawer for a month is your guaranteed ticket to ride. But airline rules should cause you to think again.

Most airlines reserve the right to cancel your confirmed reservation if you don't check in at least 10 minutes before the plane is scheduled to take off. Some airlines are much stricter, requiring you to check in a full half-hour early—or more—or you can lose your place on that flight. And there's another caveat: Most airlines require you to get all the way to the boarding gate by their check-in deadline; checking in at the airline's ticket counter usually isn't good enough.

Let's say you got to the airport in plenty of time. You've boarded the plane and stowed your carry-on luggage—but don't fasten your seat belt yet. You still can be bumped if your flight was overbooked.

U.S. Department of Transportation rules require airlines to seek out people who are willing to give up their seats before they bump anyone involuntarily. At this point, potential volunteers may be able to negotiate with the airline over what it would take to get them to relinquish their seats voluntarily. If, for example, an airline discovers that it has 110 people waiting to board a 100-passenger flight, it might offer cash or perhaps a free trip or other benefits to the first 10 volunteers. If there still aren't enough takers, it might sweeten its offer until 10 people have agreed to give up their seats on that flight.

Before you accept such an offer, find out whether the airline can confirm your seat on the next available flight. If you're put on standby, you could be stranded. You'll also want free meals and a hotel room if you have a long wait.

What if 10 people won't accept the airline's offer? In that case the airline will bump unwilling passengers—usually the last ones to get to the boarding gate. But one airline gives priority to first-class customers, even if they showed up at the last minute.

An airline that bumps you involuntarily is not required to compensate you for your inconvenience if it can arrange to get you to your destination no more than an hour late. If you will be reaching your destination between one and two hours late, however, the airline must pay you the price of your one-way ticket, with a $200 maximum. If you are going to be more than two hours late to your destination (four hours for an international flight), or if the airline doesn't make any substitute travel arrangements for you, it must pay you twice your one-way fare, with a $400 maximum.

If you're involuntarily bumped and entitled to be compensated in cash because you'll be arriving at your destination more than an hour late, you may have another opportunity to negotiate. Airlines generally would rather compensate their passengers with services than with cash, so you might, for example, be able to negotiate for a voucher for a free flight in the future in lieu of a check.

No matter what denied-boarding compensation you're offered, you always get to keep your original ticket. You can either use it on your substitute flight (you're not entitled to a free substitute flight if you've received cash compensation according to the above formula), or else you can turn it in for a refund of the price you paid for that ticket.

There are exceptions to these Department of Transportation rules. You're not entitled to compensation if you're bumped because the airline substitutes a smaller plane for the one it planned to use. The rules don't apply to charter flights or scheduled flights operated with planes that hold 60 or fewer passengers. They also don't apply to international flights inbound to the United States or to flights on U.S. or foreign airlines between two foreign cities.

Home Improvement Contracts
continued from page 2

continued from page 2

tracts that you sign in your home or at some place other than the contractor's place of business. But there are several exceptions to this rule, so you shouldn't depend on it—think before you sign.

When you do sign the contract, make only a partial payment. Never pay the full price in advance and certainly not in cash. Once the contractor says the work is completed, don't make your final payment or sign a completion certificate or receipt until the contractor has finished the work to your satisfaction, including cleanup. Once you sign, you may have surrendered many rights.

If a contractor suggests taking a mortgage or security interest in your home, ask your lawyer to look at the contract. If you grant the contractor a security interest or mortgage, there will be a lien against your home if you do not pay for the work. When a contractor takes a security interest or mortgage, federal and some state laws give you three days to change your mind and cancel the contract. Disclosures given to you before you sign the contract should explain these rights and the credit terms.

Finally, you should be aware that if a dispute does arise at any time during the project or after its completion, it may threaten your ownership of your home, even if you didn't give the contractor a security interest or mortgage and even if you have a signed release from liability to his workers and suppliers. Mechanic's lien statutes in most states will allow a contractor who hasn't been paid for the work he or she claims to have done to put a lien on your house as security for the debt. This could compromise your ability to get a home equity loan or to sell your house. See your lawyer immediately if you have such problems with your contractor.

Vol. 3, No. 1

Appendix B

OTHER SOURCES OF INFORMATION

The following firms and individuals offer services as listed for attorneys. Only those offering services relating to marketing, advertising, public relations, and total quality management initiatives are shown.

For assistance in other areas, you may wish to contact the National Association of Legal Vendors. They maintain a list of consultants and would be happy to share it with you. The NALV's address and telephone number are shown below, also.

Daniel B. Kennedy

An attorney, writer, and marketing/public relations consultant who offers a full range of marketing and public relations series to attorneys in solo practice, small firms, and large firms, as well as:

Developing effective marketing plans and strategies at all practice levels.

Creating client-focused newsletters, pamphlets, and magazines.

Attorney training and management seminars, retreats, and one-on-one coaching.

Market research and analysis.

Public relations, advertising, and creative counseling.

Ongoing support to help you meet your goals.

My writing has appeared in such periodicals and newspapers as the *ABA Journal, Life, Parents, Chicago Daily Law Bulletin, Corporate Legal Times, Art Calendar,* and *Executive Report.* I have also written three series of internationally distributed Total Quality Management newsletters for a major publishing house and have been the founding editor and publisher of two magazines.

I received my BA in English from Washington & Jefferson College and my JD, with honors, from the University of Pittsburgh School of Law where I was on the law review. I have more than 10 years of litigation practice experience in a large firm and as a sole practitioner.

I can be reached at (217)351–8595.

Altman Weil Pensa Inc.

Altman Weil Pensa is a full-service consulting firm for the legal profession, offering advice and programs on law firm marketing and management, total quality management programs, strategies, career management, technology, client surveys, partnering, malpractice prevention, and related subject areas. Although its main office is Newton Square, PA, the firm maintains satellite offices throughout the United States.

For more information, contact the firm at (215)359–9900 or write to them at Two Campus Boulevard, Newton Square, PA 19073.

Amicus Information Services

I. Barry Goldberg provides sales seminars for professionals. Contact him at (510)601–8700 or write to the company at 5900 Hollis Street, Suite R–2, Emeryville, CA 94608.

Aspen Systems Corporation

This firm provides marketing and advertising, including attorney direct mail, advice as well as programs detailing how to information management and litigation support expertise. 1600 Research Boulevard, Rockville, Maryland 20850. (301)251–5333. The firm also maintains offices in Chicago, IL; Washington, DC; and Uniondale, NY.

Business Development, Inc.

Business Development, Inc., is a Detroit-based firm that offers advice, training, and marketing support to lawyers and accountants in the United States, Canada, Europe, and Australia to assist them in developing business and improving profitability.

Julie Savarino, the founder and director of Business Development, Inc., is a member of the American Bar Association, a member of the education committee of the National Law Firm Marketing Association, and a founding member of the Professional Services Marketing Association of Michigan. In addition to her duties with BDI, Ms. Savarino, who holds an MBA from Michigan State University in finance and marketing and a law degree from the University of Detroit, is an adjunct professor at the University of Detroit Mercy Law School. There, she teaches a course on client relations and the marketing of legal services.

Business Development, Inc. may be reached at (313)963–4545.

Computer Law Systems, Inc.

Sandra G. Schley offers the programs *Win-Win Communications* and *Attracting New Clients and Cases.* Her *Win-Win Communications* program focuses, in part, on commitment to common goals and teamwork. 11000 West 78th Street, Eden Prairie, MN 55344. Phone (612)941–3801 (ext. 412).

Hildebrandt, Inc.

Hildebrandt, Inc., is a national management consulting firm that offers marketing services to small, as well as large, law firms. The firm's services focus on: positioning the firm and its lawyers; teaching marketing and sales skills; identifying client perceptions of the firm; organizing the marketing management effort; researching the most likely markets for future development; communicating with clients, prospects, and the press; and developing marketing strategies and tools. The firm's specific services, when working one-on-one with lawyers, include the following:

Marketing plan development and implementation

Training in sales, marketing, and presentation skills

Public relations and marketing communications support

Brochures

Client base analysis

Client assessment surveys

Ongoing regular advice and counsel

Hildebrandt's executive office is located in Somerville, NJ, and its other offices are located in Chicago, Dallas, Miami, and San Francisco. For more information, call (908)725–1600.

Iron Mountain Records Management

Wendy P. Shade describes her *Customer Service for the 1990s* program as a "fast-paced humorous session [that] explores both good and bad service, improvement techniques, and how to handle difficult situations and individuals." 1340 E. Sixth Street, Suite 301, Los Angeles, CA 90021. Phone (213)244–0310.

Juris, Inc.

M. Thomas Collins is available to discuss *The Pursuit of Excellence,* among other topics. At this writing, he is Chairman, National Association of Legal Vendors. His office is located at 5106 Maryland Way, Brentwood, TN 37027. (615)377–1328.

The Kilgannon Group

Rena K. Kilgannon has two programs available: *Direct Marketing to Attorneys: The Pros and Cons* and *Customer Retention and Growth: A Step by Step Program for Success.* Ms. Kilgannon can be contacted by writing to her at 3210 Peachtree Road, NE, Suite 14, Atlanta, GA 30305 or by calling her at (404)231–2140.

Law Bulletin Publishing Co.

Jeffrey L. Bryan offers programs on *Developing Client Development Programs, Helping Professionals Learn How to Sell,* and *Getting Publicity for Your Firm.* 415 N. State Street, Chicago, IL 60610. You may also call him at (312)644–7800, extension 168.

Mary Ann Walker

Ms. Walker's area of expertise is lawyer advertising. Her address is 1725 South Gaffey Street, Los Angeles, CA 90731. Call toll free: (800)454–5454.

McGrath/Power West Public Relations

Contact either Jonathan Bloom or Terri L. Foos for information on public relations programs for legal product markets. Their office is located at 3945 Freedom Circle, Suite 690, Santa Clara, CA 95054. Telephone (408)727–0351.

PCS Mailing List Company

James M. Healy can help attorneys with mailing list compilation, strategies, and analysis as well as telemarketing consultation for the legal market. Consultations are free. PCS is located at 85 Constitution Lane, Danvers, MA 01923, or phone (508)777–9161.

The National Association of Legal Vendors

The National Association of Legal Vendors is composed of firms who sell consulting services as well as computers, software, and other goods to law firms. The association has a directory of speakers available to address a number of topics of concern to attorneys and to give training programs.

More information on the NALV can be obtained by writing to its business office at 5106 Maryland Way, Brentwood, TN 37027 or by calling Dianne Lacey, Administrator, at (615)377–1328.

The National Law Firm Marketing Association

NALFMA, with more than 1,000 members, is one of the world's largest professional services marketing associations, and the premier association serving the needs of those involved in marketing for the legal profession.

Membership in the NALFMA for small firms and sole practitioners is $195 per year, with a one-time initiation fee of $100.

Included in the membership are the following:

A monthly newsletter, "Law Marketing Exchange."

Annual white papers entitled "The Law Firm Marketing Director" and "The Law Firm Marketing Department."

Annual salary survey report.

Discounts on fees for attending national and regional conferences and other services.

The white papers may be purchased by nonmembers at a cost of $20 for "The Law Firm Marketing Director" and $25 for "The Law Firm Marketing Department." The annual salary survey cost to nonmembers is $125.

Further information on NALFMA may be obtained by writing to the Executive Director, Ellen Grayce LoCurto, at 60 Revere Drive, Suite 500, Northbrook, IL 60062, or by calling (708)480–9641.

Practice Development Institute

Allan D. Koltin, a CPA, provides seminars for lawyers on a wide variety of topics. Among them are: *World Class Service—How to Get It, How to Give It, and How to Keep It; The Keys to Marketing Your Practice; How to Sell Professional Services;* and *Goal Setting for Professional Service Firms.* His offices are located at 401 N. Michigan Avenue, Suite 2600, Chicago, IL 60611–4240. His phone number is (312)245–1930 and his fax is (312)644–4423.

Rectenwald Consulting, Inc.

Jane L. Rectenwald holds an MBA from the University of Pittsburgh and a BA in English from Northwestern University. For four and one-half years, she was the Director of Marketing for Reed Smith Shaw & McClay, a large regional law firm with offices in Pittsburgh, Philadelphia, and Washington, DC. While there, she created and implemented an aggressive marketing plan for the firm's TECHLEX Group, and Reed Smith became the first law firm to receive the American Marketing Association's Marketing Excellence Award.

Jane offers clients assistance in the following areas: conducting marketing audits; creating individual attorney, department, and firm marketing plans; conducting marketing retreats; locating marketing staff or public relations and advertising agencies; and providing attorney training.

Jane has advised firms ranging in size from 5 to more than 600 lawyers. Her offices are located at 211 London Towne, Pittsburgh, PA 15226. Her telephone number is (412)488–6440. Faxes may be sent to (412)488–6442.

Index